VALE OF WHITE HORSE

THROUGH TIME

Stanley C. Jenkins

AMBERLEY PUBLISHING

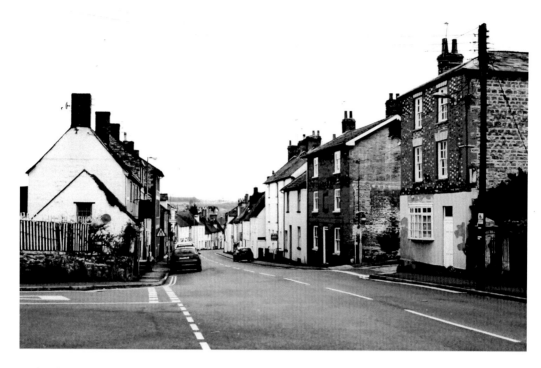

Faringdon

Faringdon is a small town in the western part of the Vale of the White Horse. It is situated on a low ridge of coral rag, which rises to about 200 feet above mean sea level on the south side of the River Thames.

First published 2013

Amberley Publishing
The Hill, Stroud, Gloucestershire, GL5 4EP
www.amberley-books.com

Copyright © Stanley C. Jenkins, 2013

The right of Stanley C. Jenkins to be identified as the
Author of this work has been asserted in accordance with
the Copyrights, Designs and Patents Act 1988.

ISBN 978 1 4456 1710 7 (print)
ISBN 978 1 4456 1719 0 (ebook)

British Library Cataloguing in Publication Data.
A catalogue record for this book is available from the
British Library.

Typesetting by Amberley Publishing.
Printed in Great Britain.

Introduction

The Vale of the White Horse is a broad tract of arable land between the Berkshire Downs and the Upper Thames, which extends from Abingdon in the east to Shrivenham in the west. The area derives its name from the famous Uffington White Horse, which is carved into a chalk hillside on White Horse Hill, the highest point of the Berkshire Downs, some 856 feet above mean sea level.

Historically, the Upper Thames Valley had been part of the Anglo-Saxon kingdom of Wessex but, following the rise of the Midland Kingdom of Mercia, the boundaries of Wessex were pushed southwards towards the chalk Downs. At length, the Thames was established as a natural boundary and thus, when the county of Berkshire was brought into existence – probably during the ninth century – the river formed a clearly defined frontier between two rival kingdoms.

In the event, the power of Mercia was thoroughly destroyed by an invasion of Danish Vikings. However, led by Alfred the Great, Wessex resisted the invaders, and in 871 the Vikings were defeated in the Battle of Ashdown, the first large-scale battle fought on open ground between the Vikings and the West Saxons. The site of the battle remains unclear, though it is generally agreed that 'Ashdown' was a generalised name for the Berkshire Downs. It was said, for many years, that the Uffington White Horse was cut into the hillside by the West Saxons to commemorate their famous victory and, although this story has been dismissed by archaeological experts, the legend is strangely persistent.

There were many further engagements between King Alfred and the Danes, and in January 878, the Danes, led by a Viking called Guthrum, launched another large-scale invasion of Wessex. Alfred was forced to take refuge in the Somerset marshes with a small party of household troops, but in the following spring he assembled a new army and defeated the Vikings at Edington, in Wiltshire. The resulting 'Treaty of Wedmore' divided England into two parts, the limit of English rule being fixed along the line of Watling Street.

As a corollary of these events, the remaining parts of Mercia between Watling Street and the Thames were incorporated into greater Wessex, and the West Saxon shire system was applied to Mercia and other parts of the country as Alfred and his children consolidated their control over the rest of England – Oxfordshire being brought into existence during the early tenth century.

This fairly detailed introduction is necessary because it explains and underlines the historic distinction between Berkshire and 'The Vale of the White Horse', which were regarded as Wessex territory on the south side of the Thames, and Oxfordshire to the north, which was, for a time, under Mercian control.

Major changes ensued in 1974 when, as part of a highly controversial local government reorganisation scheme, a large part of north Berkshire, encompassing eighty-one parishes, was transferred from Berkshire to Oxfordshire. As part of this process, the Borough of Abingdon, the Urban District of Wantage, the Rural District of Abingdon, the Rural District of Faringdon, and part of the Rural District of Wantage were combined to form a new local government district known as 'The Vale of White Horse', while the Wallingford Rural District (including Didcot) became part of the newly created South Oxfordshire District.

A minor complication arises in that the boundaries of 'The Vale of White Horse' local government district do not necessarily correspond with those of the geographic Vale of the White Horse; Appleford-on-Thames, for example, is included within the present local government boundary, although the village is somewhat further to the east of the geographic Vale. Appleford and neighbouring villages such as Little Wittenham and Long Wittenham nevertheless have many affinities with the Vale in terms of history, architecture and scenery, and it is appropriate to include them in this present study, which applies the term 'The Vale of the White Horse' in its broadest sense in order to describe the part of Berkshire between the Thames and the Berkshire Downs that now belongs to Oxfordshire.

Acknowledgements

Thanks are due to Diana Lydiard and Martin Loader for help with the supply of photographs for this book. Other images were obtained from the Lens of Sutton Collection, the Witney & District Museum and from the author's own collection.

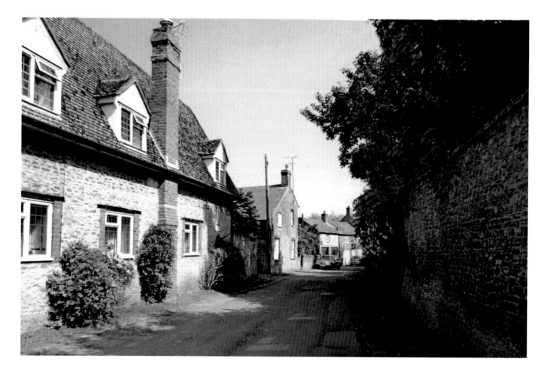

Longworth
Longworth is one of a number of villages sited along the coral rag ridge on the south side of the Thames and, like other villages in what was once north Berkshire, its houses and cottages are mainly of stone construction.

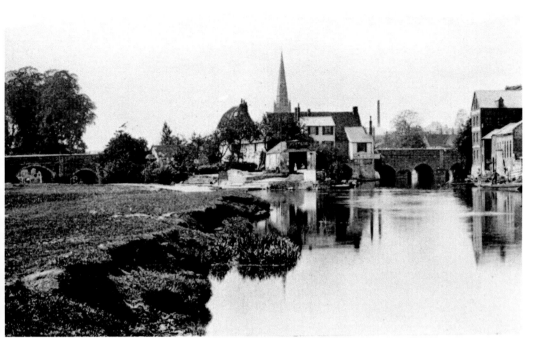

Abingdon: A Riverside Town

Situated on the River Thames near its junction with the River Ock, Abingdon was traditionally regarded as one of the most interesting and historic towns in Berkshire – although it is now, of course, part of Oxfordshire! The town boasts an attractive riverside frontage, as shown in this postcard view of around 1912, which is looking west towards Abingdon Bridge. The colour photograph was taken from the cabin roof of the narrow boat *Towy*, some eighty years later.

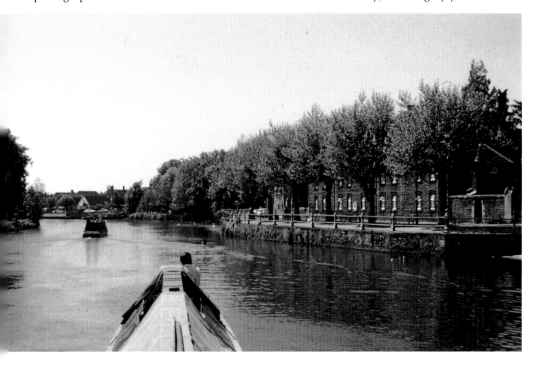

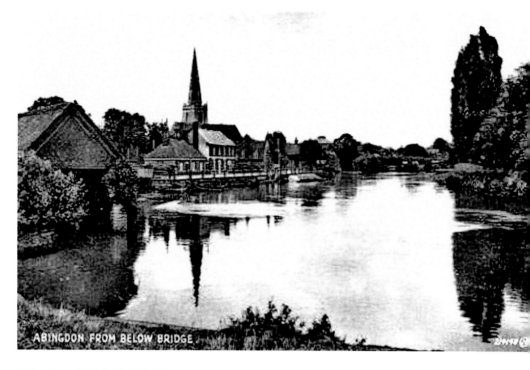

Abingdon: St Helen's Wharf

These two views show a group of old riverside buildings on the west side of the river, including the Anchor Inn and the neighbouring Christ's Hospital almshouses, with St Helen's church visible in the background. The sepia view is from an early twentieth-century postcard, while the colour photograph was taken in the 1980s.

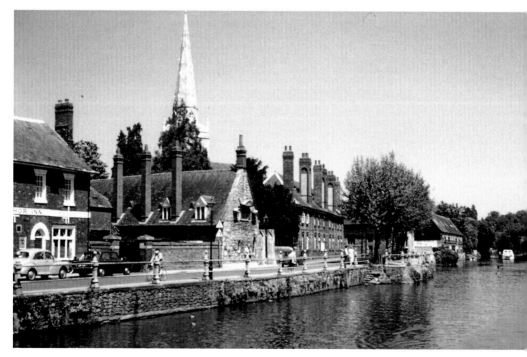

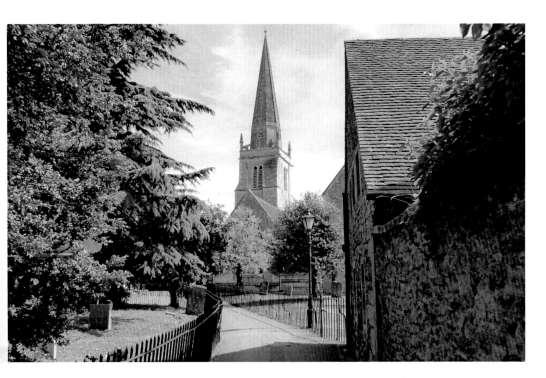

Abingdon: St Helen's Church

This large, urban church boasts a nave with double aisles on either side, the result being an unusually wide and spacious building with five parallel aisles. The two northernmost aisles are the earliest, while the present chancel and the inner south aisle were built when the church was reconstructed during the fifteenth century. The outer south aisle was added in 1539 under the terms of the will of Katherine Audlett, widow of John Audlett, the Steward of Abingdon Abbey. The north-east tower is in the Early English style and dates from the thirteenth century, although the spire was added in the fifteenth century. The old print depicts the church and neighbouring buildings from the river during the mid-nineteenth century. The colour photograph, in contrast, was taken from the churchyard in July 2013.

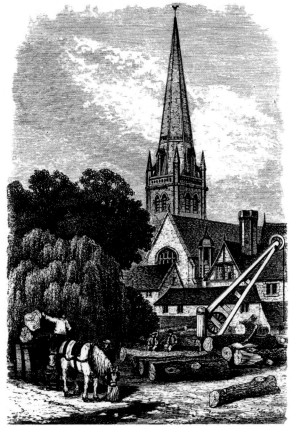

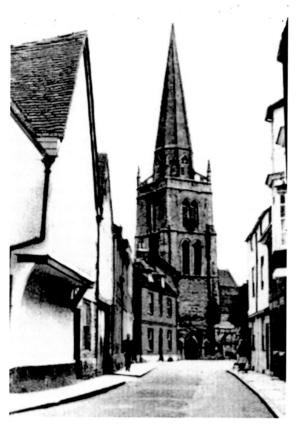

Abingdon: East St Helen Street

The upper view, from an Edwardian colour-tinted postcard, is looking southwards along East St Helen Street during the early years of the twentieth century. St Helen's church features prominently in the background, while timber-framed buildings can be seen to the left. The colour photograph, taken from a similar vantage point in July 2013, reveals that little has changed in this part of Abingdon.

Although many of the buildings in this street are of eighteenth- or nineteenth-century origin, others are much older; the gabled houses that can be seen to the left in both pictures probably date from the seventeenth century. One or two properties were demolished during the 1960s, but otherwise East St Helen Street remains one of the most unspoiled streets in Abingdon.

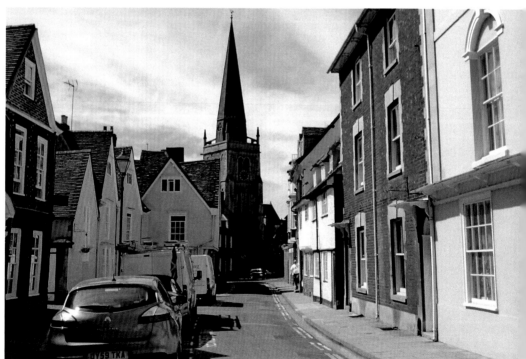

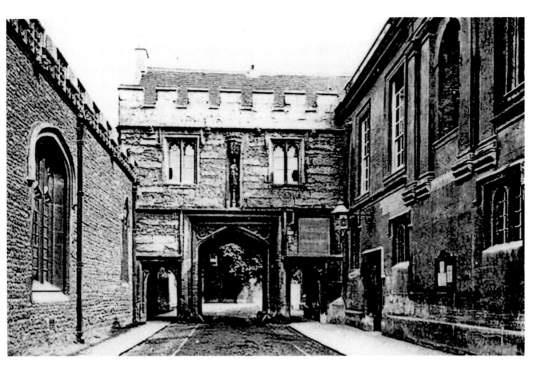

Abingdon: The Abbey

Founded in 675, Abingdon Abbey was destroyed by the Danes during the Viking wars, but it was subsequently rebuilt and, in the medieval period, this Benedictine foundation exerted great power and influence. The last abbot, Thomas Rowland, surrendered the abbey to Thomas Cromwell in February 1539 and most of the buildings were later demolished. Abbot Rowland, the Prior, and twenty-four other monks received pensions, the abbot being awarded the very generous sum of £200 per annum.

The principal remains comprise the abbey gatehouse and the adjoining church of St Nicholas, together with some of the former domestic buildings, including the Prior's Lodging and a lengthy, two-storey building known as the Guest House (now known as the Long Gallery). The upper view, from an old postcard, shows Abbey Gatehouse, while the lower photograph provides a glimpse of the Prior's Lodging during the early 1920s. The elaborate hooded chimney is an interesting feature.

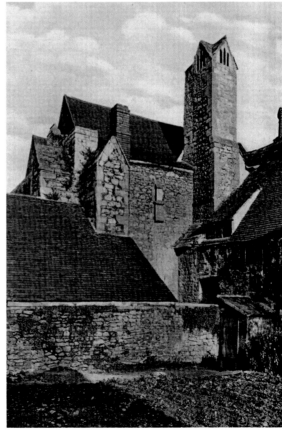

9

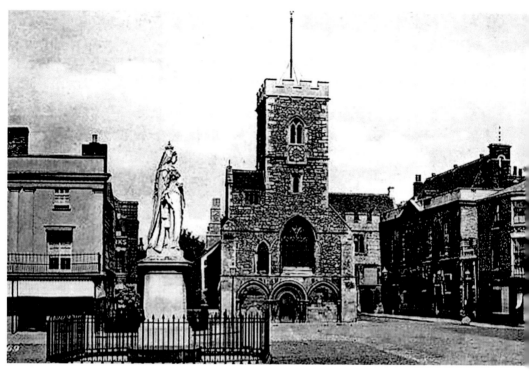

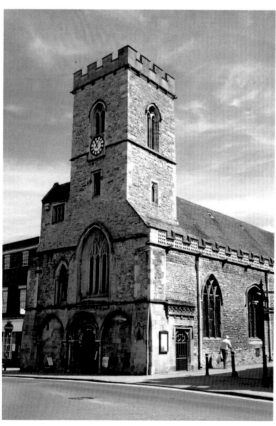

Abingdon: The Church of St Nicholas

Sited next to the Abbey Gatehouse, St Nicholas church was originally a chapel for lay workers at the abbey. The church was damaged in 1327 when the abbey was attacked and plundered by local townsfolk in connection with a protracted dispute about market rights. The chancel was damaged in an arson attack in 1953, as a result of which the organ was destroyed.

The most interesting feature of the church is perhaps the gabled turret on the north-west corner of the tower, which can be seen in the accompanying photographs; it contains a spiral staircase leading to an upper room. The sepia postcard view dates from around 1912, and the colour photograph was taken in July 2013. The statue of Queen Victoria, which can be seen in the earlier picture, was unveiled in 1887 to mark the Queen's Golden Jubilee. It was moved to the Abbey Grounds in 1946.

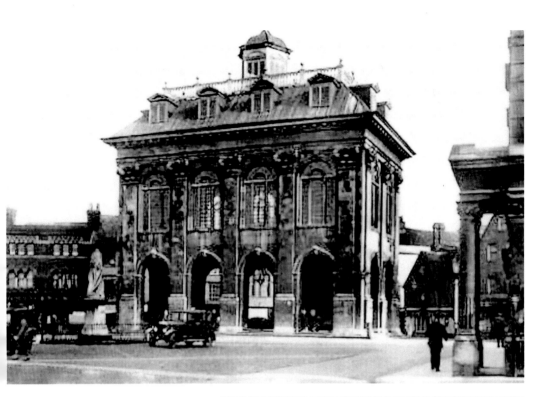

Abingdon: The County Hall

Occupying a prominent position in the Market Place, Abingdon's monumental County Hall (now a museum) was built in the 1670s. The architect was probably Christopher Kempster (1627–1715) of Burford, a local stonemason, quarry-owner and architect who had trained under Christopher Wren. This impressive Baroque building consists of a raised council chamber above an open marketing area, together with attics and a cellar. The sepia postcard dates from around 1928, and the recent colour view was taken from a slightly different vantage point in July 2013.

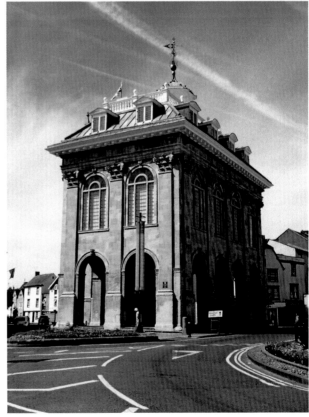

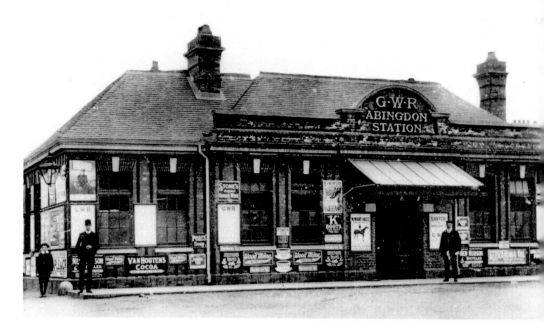

Abingdon: The Railway Station

The Abingdon Railway was opened from 'Abingdon Junction' to Abingdon, a distance of 1 mile 70 chains, on 2 June 1856. The line, originally broad gauge, was converted to standard gauge in 1872, and at the same time the old junction was abolished and the branch was extended northwards, alongside the GWR main line to Radley. Passenger services were withdrawn in 1963, but goods traffic continued until 1984. The upper view shows the terminal building around 1912, while the lower view shows part of the redeveloped station site in 2013.

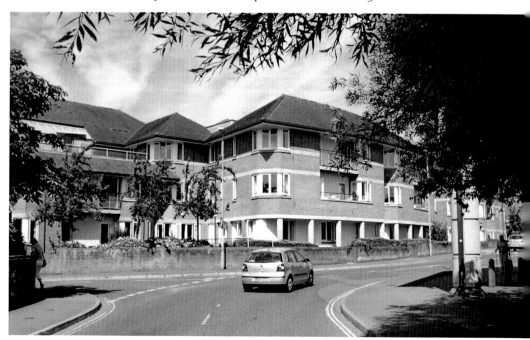

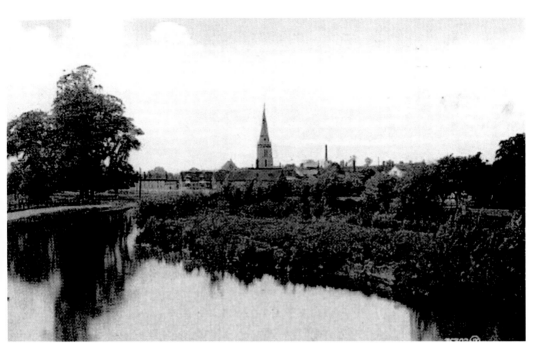

Abingdon: A Final Glimpse

It is interesting to reflect that Abingdon, the headquarters of the Vale of White Horse local government district, was once the county town of Berkshire. These two final views provide glimpses of Abingdon from the river around 1912, and a century later in 2013. Further details of this historic Thameside town can be found in *Abingdon Through Time* by Pamela Horn (Amberley: 2009).

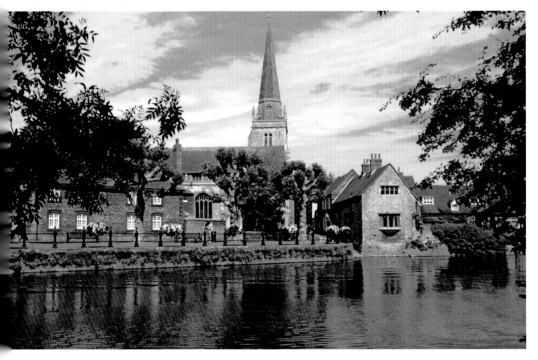

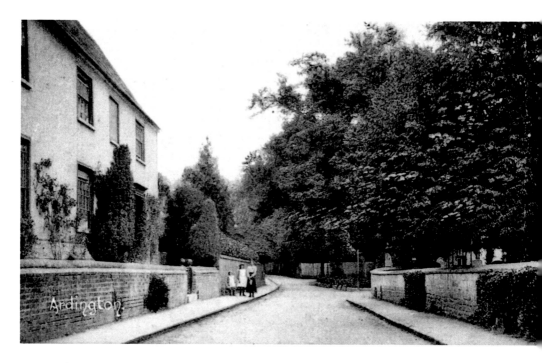

Ardington: The Vicarage

Ardington, a small village about 2 miles to the east of Wantage, is a classic 'estate' village. Many of the substantial Victorian cottages were built by Robert Lloyd Lindsay (1832–1901), who had won the VC during the Crimean War. In 1858, he married Harriet Lloyd, the daughter of a wealthy industrialist, who purchased the nearby Lockinge estate as a wedding present for the happy couple. The pictures show part of Church Street around 1912 and in 2013, with the churchyard wall visible to the right.

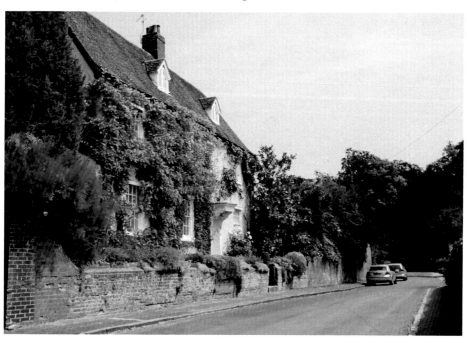

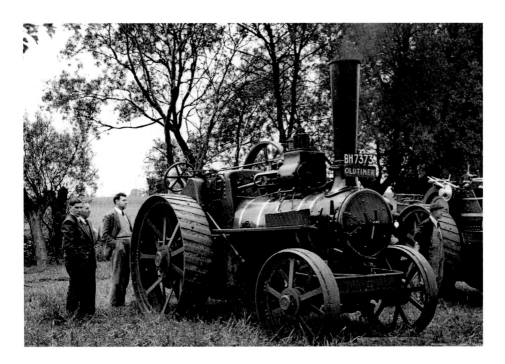

Appleford-on-Thames

Situated about 3 miles south-east of Abingdon, Appleford consists chiefly of two main streets, one of which is Main Road, while the other is Church Street. In 1950, Appleford became the birthplace of the traction engine preservation movement when local farmer Arthur Napper arranged a race between his engine *Old Timer* and *Ladygrove* – an engine owned by a fellow enthusiast. Thereafter, traction engine rallies were regularly held in the village. The upper picture shows *Old Timer* in the 1950s, and the lower view shows the village green in 2013.

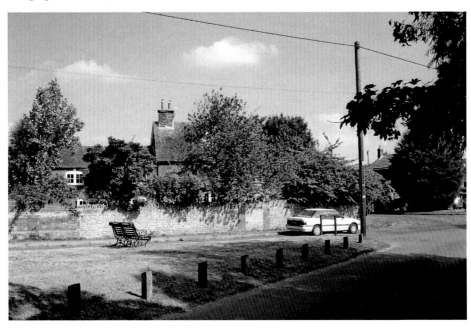

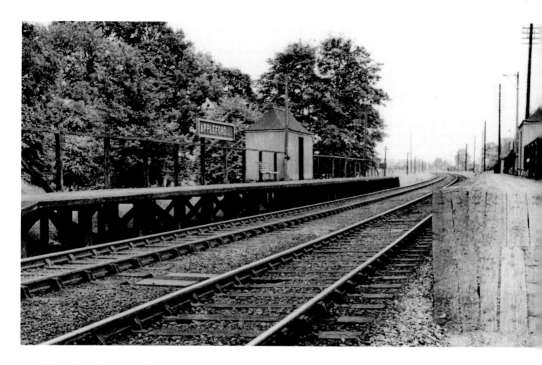

Appleford-on-Thames: The Halt

Appleford residents still enjoy the benefits of a rail service. Appleford Halt was opened by GWR on 11 September 1933 as an unstaffed stopping place on the Didcot to Oxford line. It was originally equipped with characteristic Great Western 'pagoda' shelters, as seen in the upper photograph, which was taken during the 1960s and is looking south towards Didcot. The recent picture shows a northbound 'Voyager' unit passing beneath the road overbridge at the north end of the platforms.

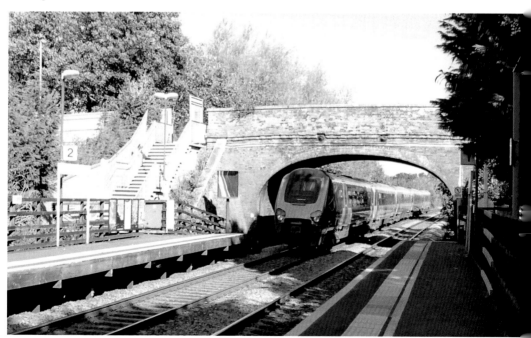

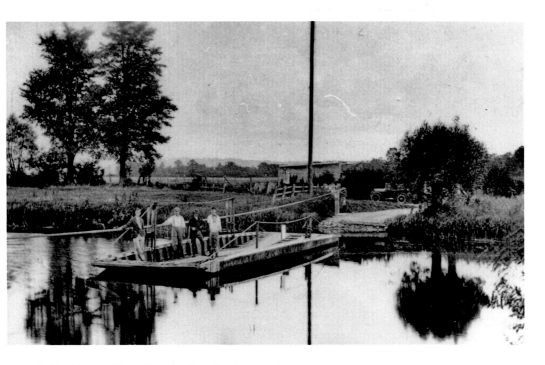

Bablockhythe: 'Crossing the Stripling Thames'

Bablockhythe, some 11 miles 4 chains upstream from Oxford, was once the site of a vehicular ferry, which features in Matthew Arnold's poem 'The Scholar Gipsy'. Although this quaint old feature has long since disappeared, a pedestrian ferry still operates sporadically at the adjacent Ferryman Inn. The upper picture shows the ferry around 1920, while the colour photograph was taken from more or less the same position in July 2013.

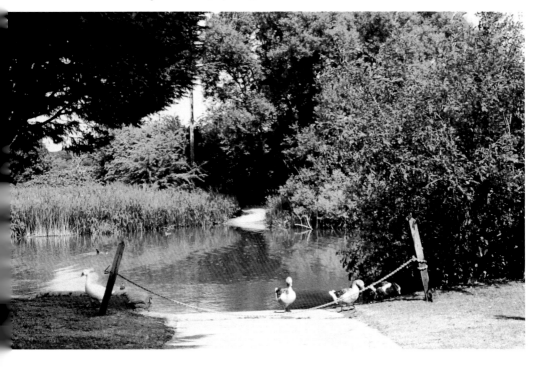

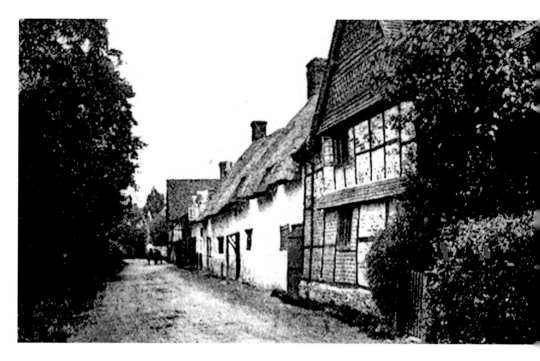

Blewbury: Westbrook Street

Blewbury is a very attractive village lying under the slope of the Berkshire Downs, about 3 miles to the south of Didcot. It contains numerous seventeenth- and eighteenth-century houses and cottages, as exemplified by these examples in Westbrook Street. The upper view is from a postcard of around 1910, while the colour photograph was taken in 2013. The house on the extreme right is of timber-framed construction, but the panels between its timbers are filled by brickwork, a building technique known as 'brick nogging'.

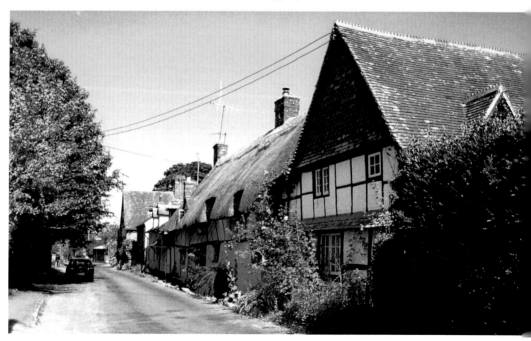

Blewbury: The Cleve

The upper picture depicts part of the labyrinthine network of paths and streams that criss-cross the centre of Blewbury. In earlier days, the village contained numerous cress beds – watercress cultivation being a significant local activity in many of the local villages. The cress beds were fed by springs that emerge along the foot of the Downs. The lower view, taken in a back lane that bears the odd name 'Nottingham Fee', shows a seventeenth-century, timber-framed dwelling, formerly a farmhouse, known as 'Great Tree'. Again, brick nogging is the predominant form of construction. The name 'Nottingham Fee' is presumably derived from the Nottingham family, who own land in the village during the medieval period.

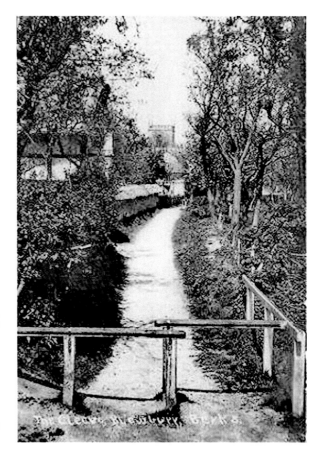

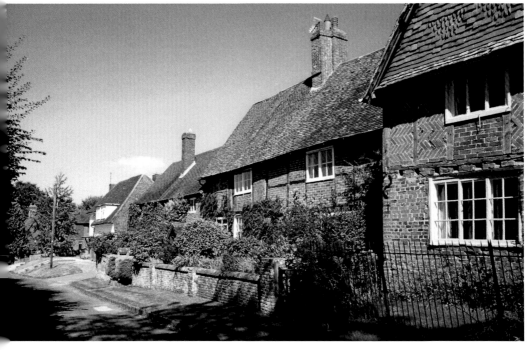

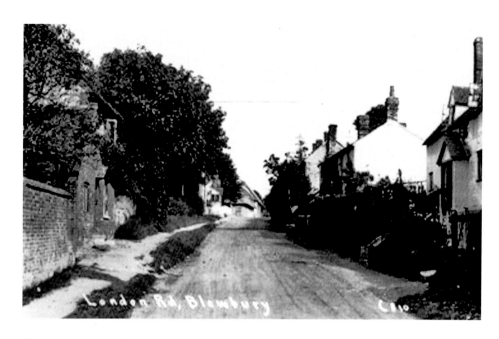

Blewbury: London Road

The upper view is looking eastwards along London Road, which skirts the southern edge of the village. This busy thoroughfare, now the busy A417, contains a number of interesting old buildings, including the house shown in the lower photograph. This timer-framed structure is of 'close-studded' construction with tall, narrow panels, as opposed to the squarish 'box-frame' panels that can be seen on the house in Nottingham Fee.

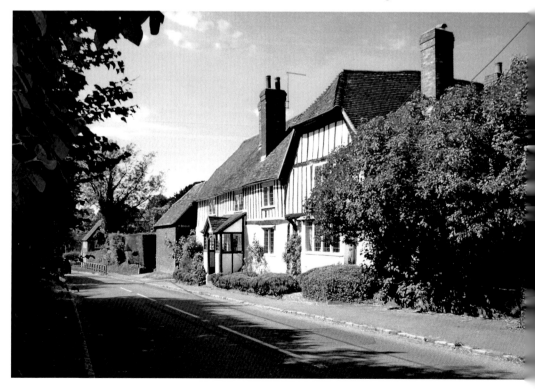

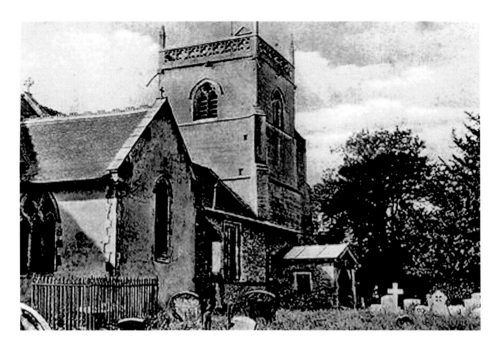

Blewbury: St Michael's Church

The parish church has a complex history. The original Norman building was enlarged during the twelfth century, when transepts and a central tower were added, but the resulting cruciform plan was modified when aisles were added on either side of the nave, the south transept being extended eastwards to form a chapel. In a subsequent modification, the original tower was dismantled and a new tower was added at the west end. The accompanying illustrations show the church from the north around 1912, and from the south in 2013.

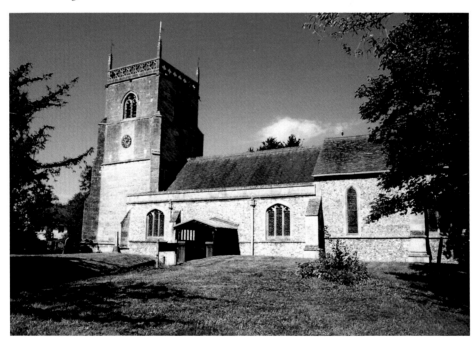

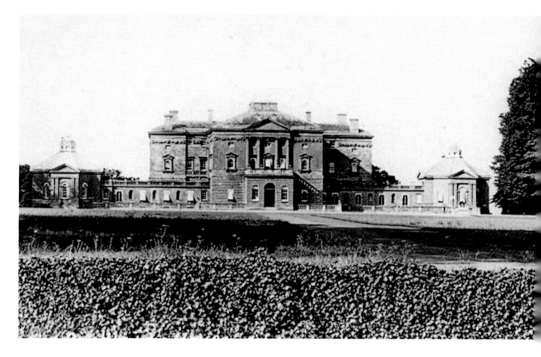

Buckland

Buckland is situated about a mile to the south of the River Thames and, like neighbouring villages, it contains many picturesque old cottages, most of which were constructed of local stone. Buckland House, to the west of the village, was formerly the home of the Throckmorton family. It was designed by John Wood (1728–1781) of Bath, and built in 1757. The upper view shows this Palladian mansion around 1912, and the colour photograph was taken over ninety years later.

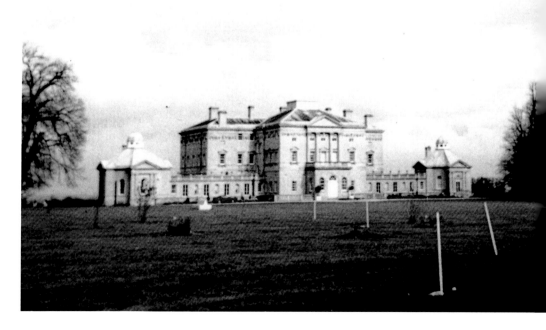

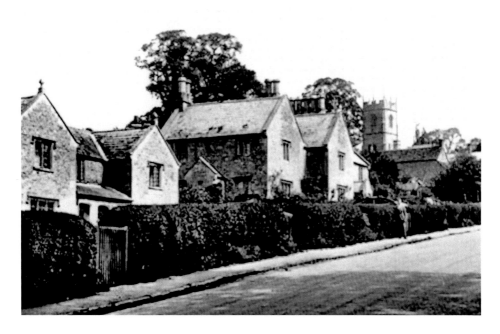

Coleshill Village

Sited near the Wiltshire border, roughly midway between Faringdon and Highworth, Coleshill was another typical estate village, many of the villagers being employed on the Coleshill estate. In 1940, Coleshill House became a highly secretive training centre for an elite force known as the 'Auxiliary Units', which would have provided a last-ditch defence in the event of a German invasion. The sepia view depicts part of the main street, possibly around 1920, while the colour photograph was taken from a position slightly in further to the east in 2013.

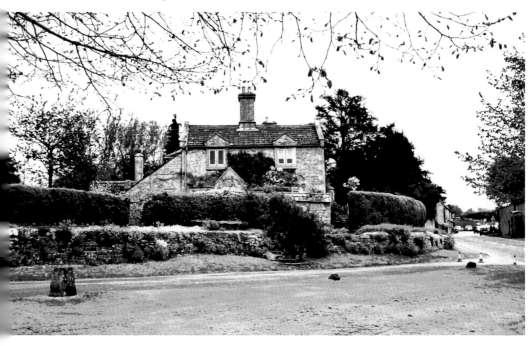

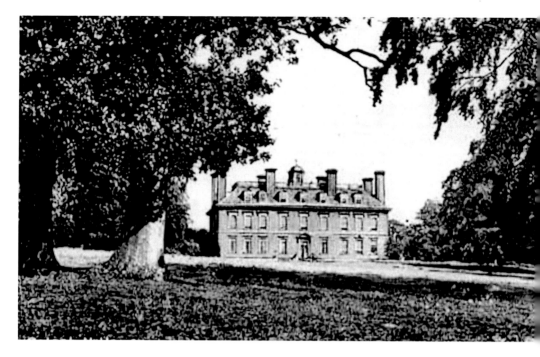

Coleshill House

Designed by Sir Roger Pratt (1620–85), Coleshill House was built in the 1650s. The building was of two storeys, with a half-sunk basement and dormered attics, its simple, yet dignified, appearance reflecting the architectural taste of the Commonwealth period. Sadly, Coleshill House was accidentally set on fire by a builder's blow-lamp in 1952 and, despite the efforts of villagers and firemen, this historic property was destroyed. The upper view shows the building around 1912, while the lower view shows the main gateposts in 2013.

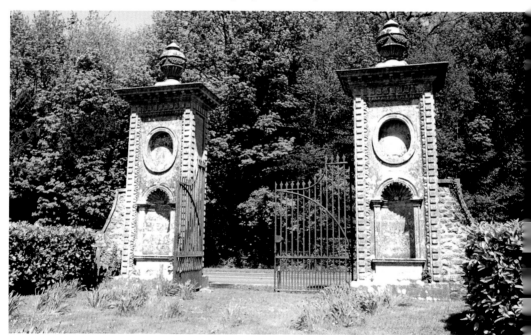

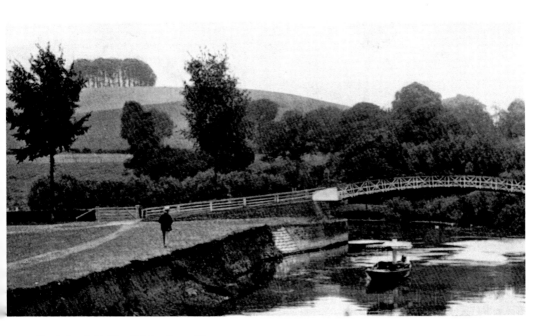

Day's Lock & The Wittenham Clumps

Day's Lock, 16 miles 6 chains downstream from Oxford, is situated on the River Thames near Little Wittenham. It was built in 1789, and the lock chamber is 154 feet in length. The upper picture dates from around 1912, and the recent colour view was taken in September 2013. The Wittenham Clumps, which can be seen in the photographs, are two conspicuous landmarks beside the Thames. Sinodun, the easternmost hill, is the site of an ancient hill fort.

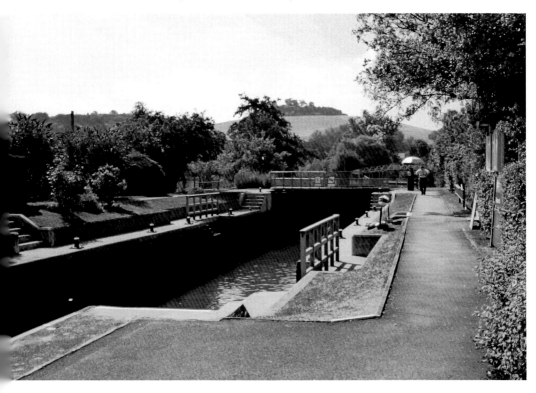

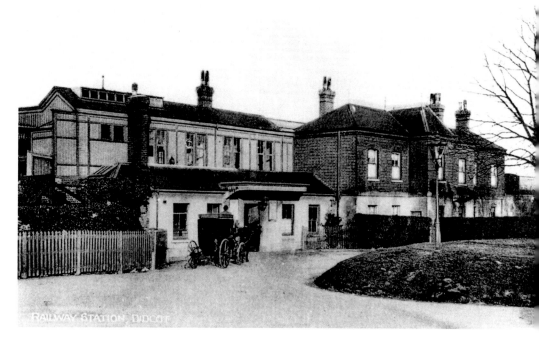

Didcot: The Railway Station

At the start of the Victorian period Didcot was merely a village, but its fortunes were transformed by the opening of the Great Western Railway main line on 1 June 1840, and the opening of the Oxford line on 12 June 1844. Didcot subsequently developed as an important railway junction with an impressive range of facilities, including marshalling sidings and busy engine sheds, as well as an important passenger station. The lower view dates from around 1912, while the colour photograph was taken in 2013.

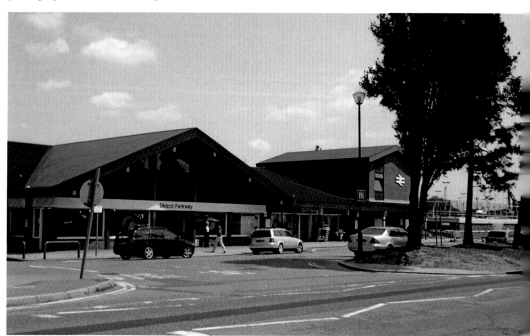

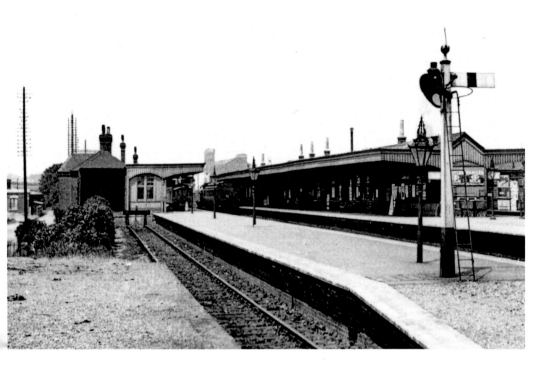

Didcot: The Railway Station

There were, at one time, seven platforms at Didcot, including two terminal bays on the south side of the station, but these were removed in 1965, leaving five lengthy through platforms in situ. The platforms are numbered in logical sequence from one to five, and the upper view is looking westwards along what is now Platform One, around 1912. The recent photograph was taken from Platform Five, and it shows a class '66' locomotive, with Didcot Power Station visible in the background.

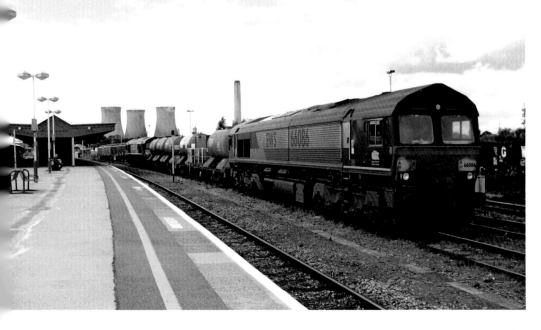

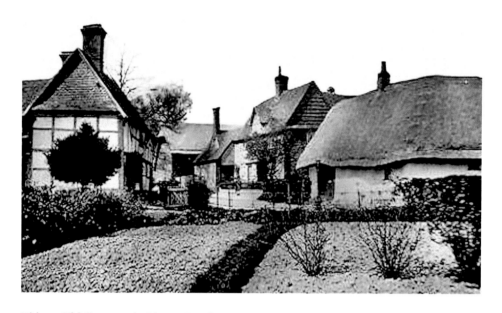

Didcot: Old Cottages in Manor Road

Writing in the 1911 *Little Guide to Berkshire*, Frederick G. Brabant (1856–1929) complained that Didcot would 'be only too well-known as a junction on the GWR which all of the better expresses carefully avoid'. However, the old village, 'just five minutes' walk from the grimy railway station', was a 'rural Arcadia' with a 'peaceful, old-world character'. This old postcard view shows the village as F. G. Brabant would have known it, while the colour photograph shows this still tranquil corner of Didcot in July 2013.

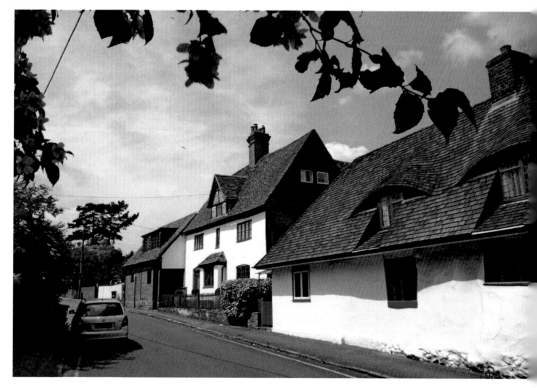

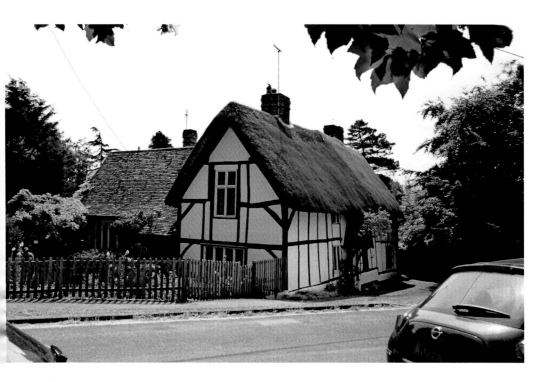

Didcot: Rectory Cottages

This old house in Lydalls Road dates back to the seventeenth century. It is of box-frame construction – a building technique found throughout the Vale of the White Horse. The rear wing, with its curious pointed cupola, was adapted for use as a school by the Victorian architect Charles Buckeridge (1832–73). The colour photograph was taken in July 2013, while the sepia postcard view provides a glimpse of the building during the early years of the twentieth century.

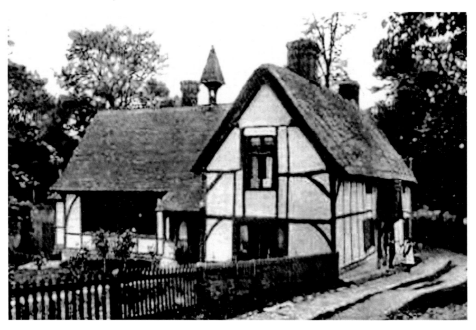

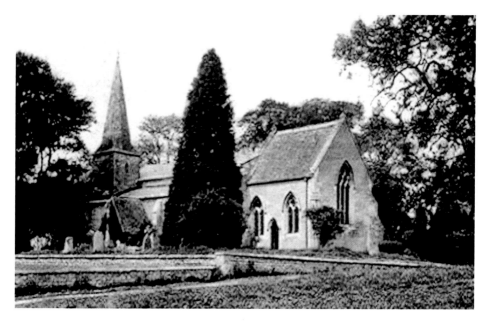

Didcot: All Saints Church

The parish church consists of a nave, chancel, west tower, porch and aisles, the porch and north aisles being Victorian additions, although the rest of the building dates back to the late Decorated Period of the mid-fourteenth century. The wooden tower, which was reconstructed during the nineteenth century, is supported by an internal timber frame at the west end of the south aisle. The accompanying photographs show the church around 1912, and in the summer of 2013.

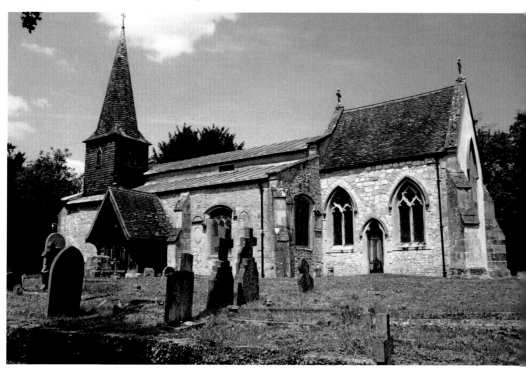

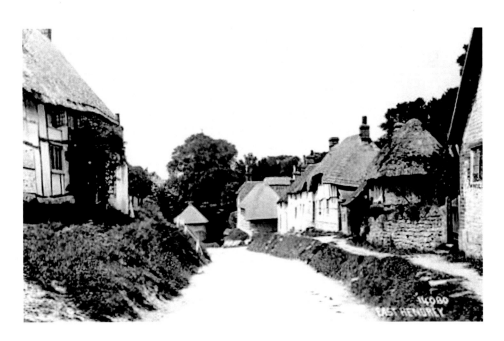

East Hendred: Old Buildings in Newbury Road

Situated about 4 miles to the west of Didcot, East Hendred was once a centre of the cloth trade. It is now merely a village, though it contains many interesting old timber-framed buildings, which serve as tangible reminders of former prosperity. The sepia view, from a postcard dating from around 1912, is looking northwards along Newbury Road, while the recent colour photograph, taken in July 2013, shows another group of cottage in a different part of the same street.

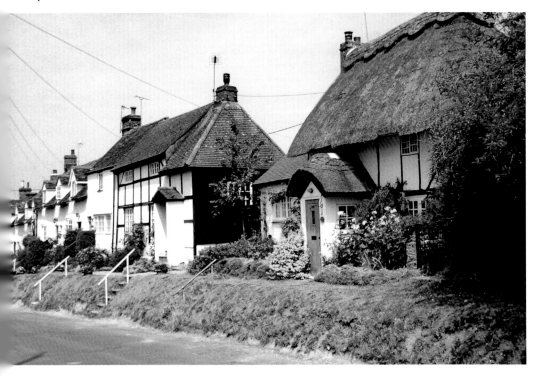

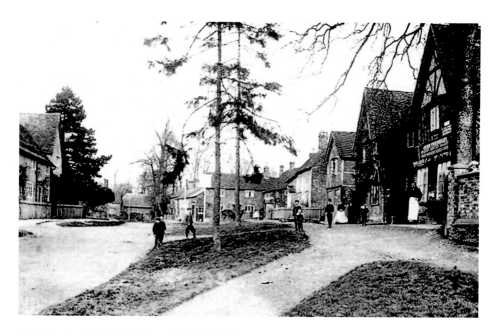

East Hendred: Old Buildings in the High Street

Above: Newbury Road merges imperceptibly with the High Street to form the main village street. The upper view is looking northwards along the High Street during the Edwardian period. The large timber-framed building that can be seen to the right of the picture incorporates a mixture of close-studding and brickwork nogging, the bricks in this instance being laid in a decorative 'herring-bone' pattern. *Below*: A recent photograph, taken from a similar vantage point in July 2013.

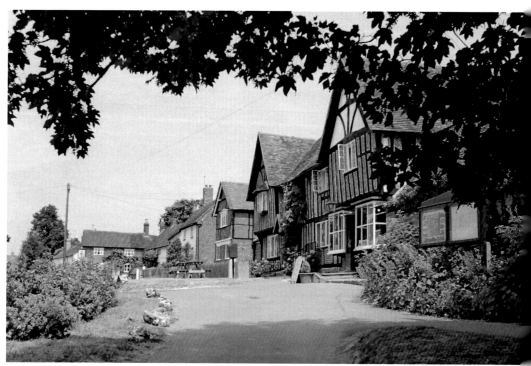

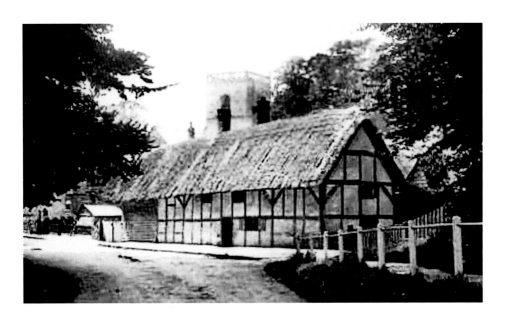

East Hendred: The High Street – Spark's Farmhouse
Above: An Edwardian postcard view showing Spark's Farmhouse, which is situated at the southern end of High Street, near its end-on junction with Newbury Road. This sixteenth-century structure is of box-frame construction, with roughcast infilling and a thatched roof. The south end of the building is weather-boarded, suggesting that it was used for agricultural purposes. *Below*: A recent view, showing the building in excellent condition in July 2013.

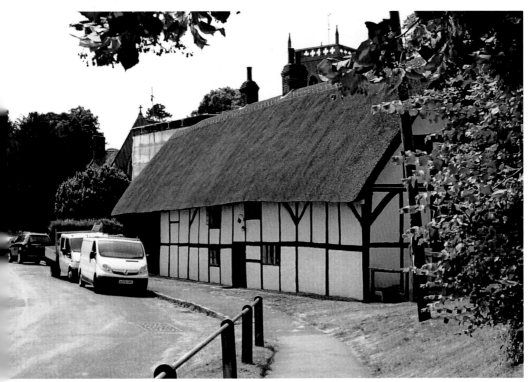

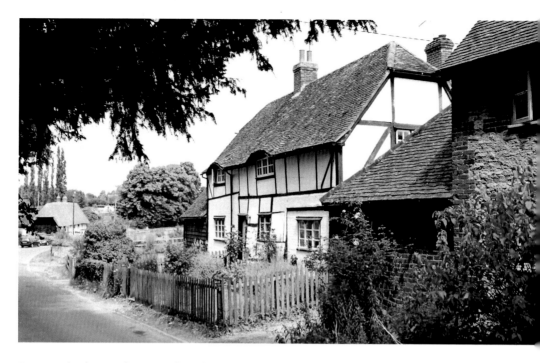

East Hendred – Newbury Road & Church Street

Above: Another typical box-framed cottage at the lower end of Newbury Road; Spark's Farmhouse can be glimpsed in the distance. *Below*: The church of St Augustine of Canterbury, comprising a nave, north aisle, chancel, north transept, south chapel and west tower, together with two south aisles, contains Early English features, although many of the windows reflect the Decorated style. The building was restored by the architect Henry Woodyer (1816–96) in 1860/61; both of these photographs were taken in 2013. *Inset*: cottages in Church Street.

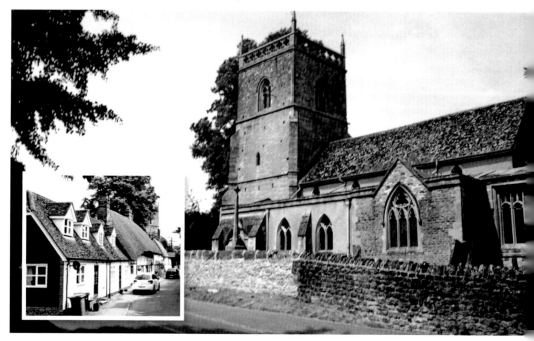

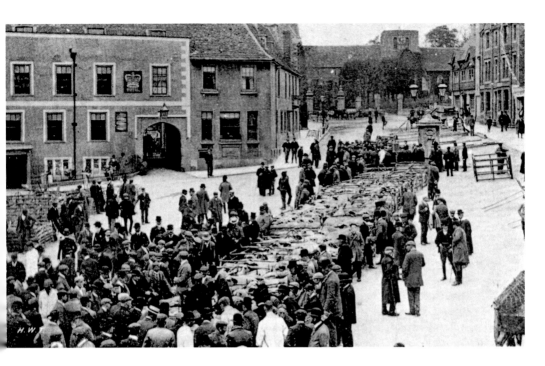

Faringdon: The Market Place

The Domesday Book records that in 1086, 'Ferendone', a royal manor of thirty hides, contained forty-five households, including seventeen *villani* (villagers), twelve *bordarii* (smallholders) and sixteen *servi* (serfs), suggesting a population of around 200. A weekly market was granted by Henry III in 1218, and this was confirmed by Edward III in 1313. The upper picture provides a glimpse of the Market Place, looking northwards on a busy market day around 1900, while the colour photograph is looking south from the churchyard in 2013.

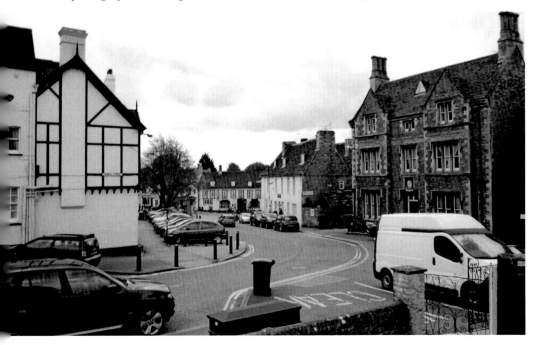

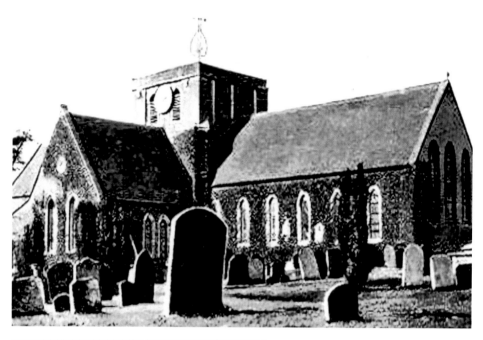

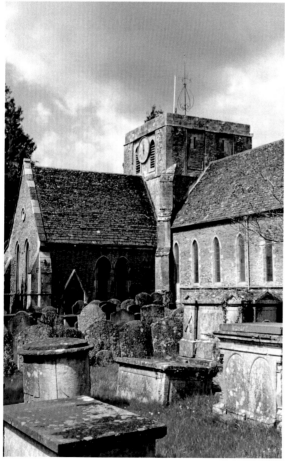

Faringdon: All Saints Church
The parish church is a cruciform structure with a central tower. Its architectural features reflect the 'Transitional' and Early English periods, suggesting that the present building was constructed during the late twelfth and early thirteenth centuries. In 1644, Faringdon was occupied by Royalist forces, prompting a raid by Oliver Cromwell in April 1645, and a further attack by Sir Robert Pye (1622–1701) in the following year. Sir Robert, a prominent local Parliamentarian who had married John Hampden's sister, had the satisfaction of ejecting the Royalists from Faringdon House, which had, prior to the war, been his own home. During the course of these operations, the church was damaged by artillery fire and the spire was destroyed – which explains the present 'stumpy' appearance of the tower!

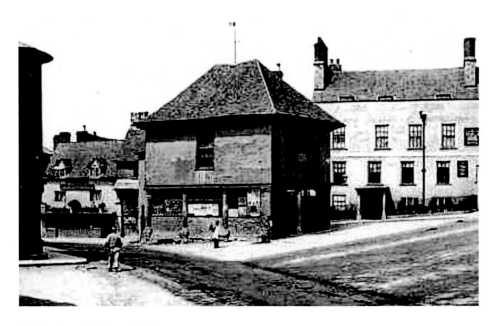

Faringdon: The Town Hall

Occupying a prominent position at the west end of the Market Place, the Old Town Hall is a seventeenth-century structure with a hipped roof. The council chamber, on the first floor, is supported upon Tuscan columns, the ground floor being an open loggia. This picturesque building was used as a library for several years, but it has now been restored as a public meeting room. The upper view dates from around 1912, while the colour picture was taken in May 2013.

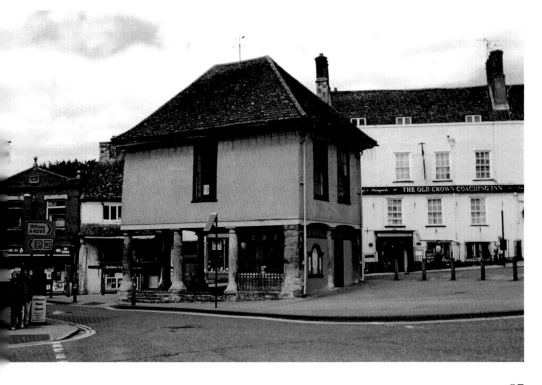

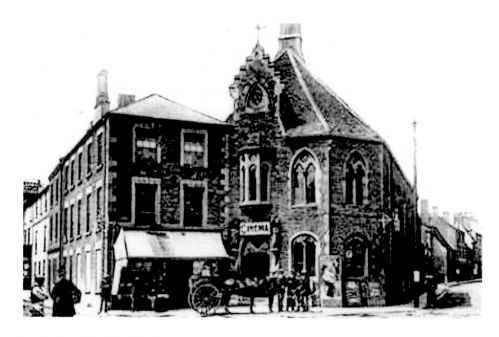

Faringdon: The Corn Exchange

Situated in the 'Cornmarket' at the west end of the Market Place, Faringdon's Victorian-Gothic Corn Exchange was erected by a private company and opened in 1863; it stands on the site of the the Green Dragon Inn. The building later became a cinema, although it was purchased by the local authorities in 1935 for use as a public hall. The upper view dates from around 1920, while the colour photograph was taken in May 2013. Gloucester Street can be seen to the right.

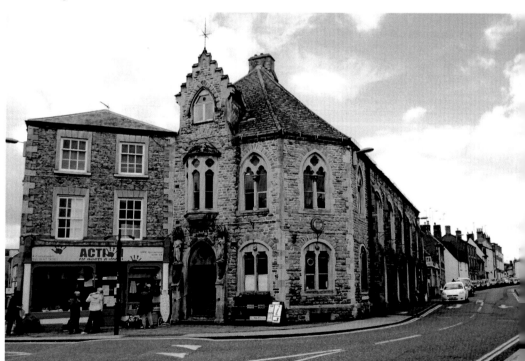

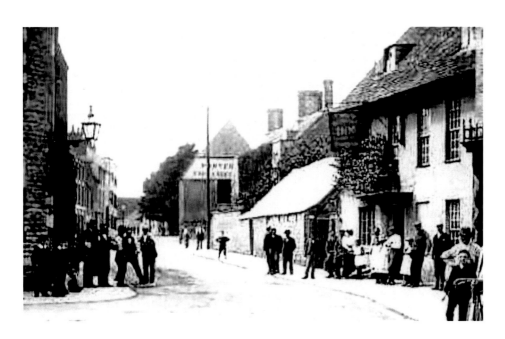

Faringdon: Gloucester Street

Above: An Edwardian postcard view of Gloucester Street, which extends due west from the Cornmarket. *Below*: A recent photograph, taken from a similar vantage point in May 2013. The Volunteer Inn, which can be seen to right in both pictures, probably dates from the mid-eighteenth century, while the Corn Exchange can be seen to the left of the picture.

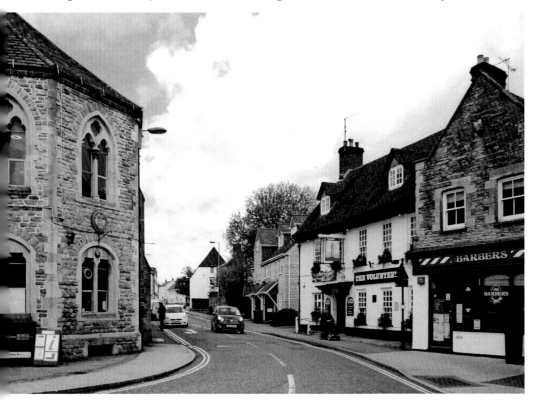

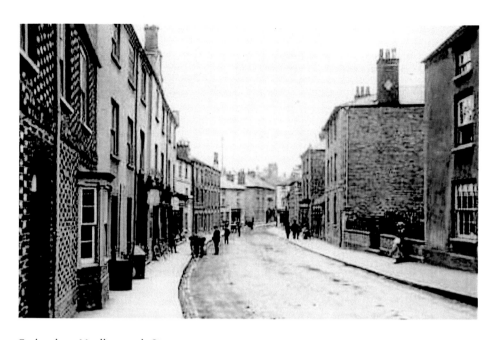

Faringdon: Marlborough Street

Two views of Marlborough Street. The upper picture is looking north-east towards the Cornmarket during the early years of the twentieth century, while the recent colour photograph is looking south-westwards in the opposite direction. Although there has been a certain amount of demolition, most of the properties that can be seen in the older view have survived. The Red Lion, on the extreme left of the lower picture, is a seventeenth-century structure with bay windows at the front and extensive outbuildings at the rear.

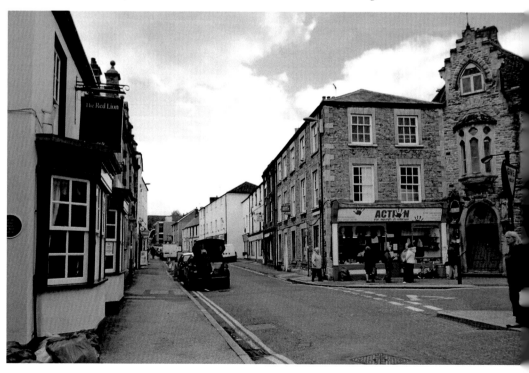

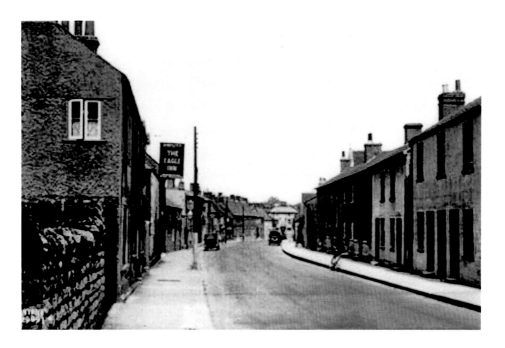

Faringdon: Coxwell Street

Forming, in effect, a south-westwards continuation of Marlborough Street, Coxwell Street (now the B4019) is a residential street that dates mainly from the nineteenth century. The Eagle Inn, which can be seen to the left in both pictures, is now a private dwelling. Other now-closed pubs in Coxwell Street include the Gardener's Arms and the Queen's Head.

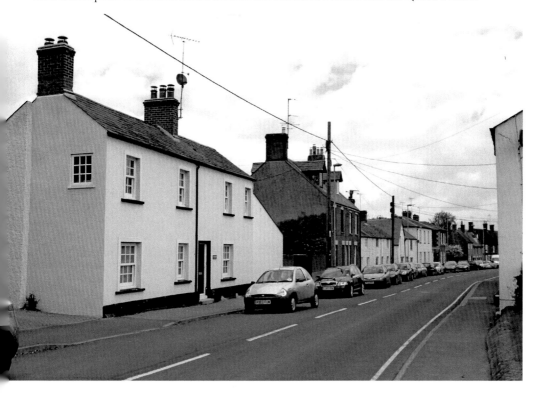

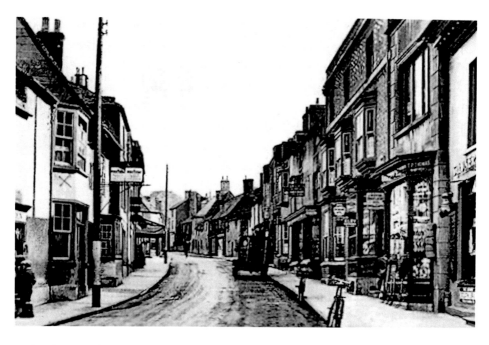

Faringdon: London Street Looking Eastwards

London Street, which extends east-north-eastwards from the Market Place, was also known as Bull Street. The photographs reveal that, in contrast to Abingdon and Wantage, Faringdon is built predominantly of local stone, although some of the buildings are of red-brick construction, and many are attractively colour-washed in cream or blue.

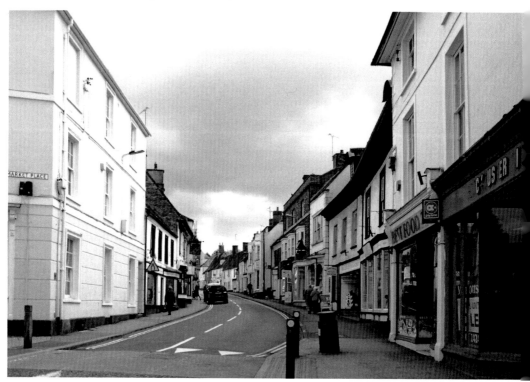

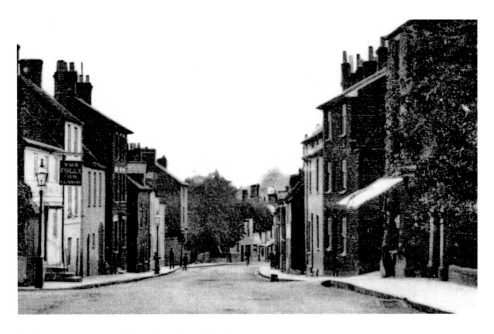

Faringdon: London Street Looking Westwards

These two photographs are both looking westwards along London Street from its junction with Coach Lane and Stanford Road. No. 54, the Folly Inn, which can be seen to the left, is now the Folly House. The pub derived its name from the nearby Faringdon Folly, a 140-foot brick tower erected in 1935 by Gerald Tyrwhitt-Wilson, the eccentric 14th Baron Berners (1884–1950). A notice outside the folly warned that 'Members of the Public committing suicide from this tower do so entirely at their own risk'!

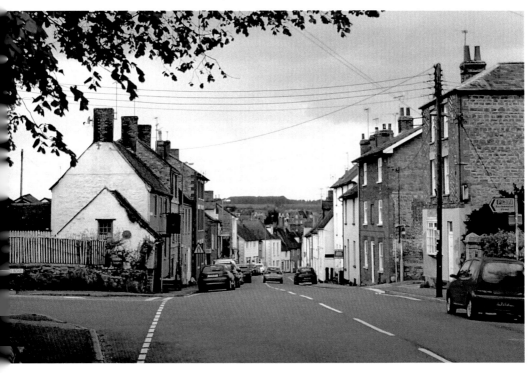

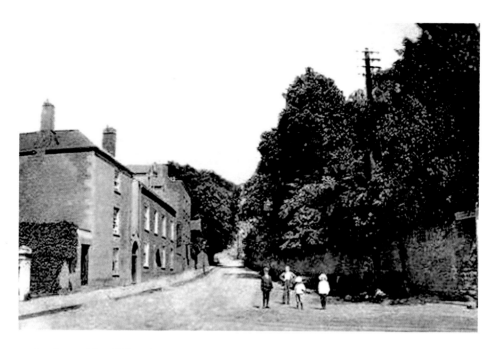

Faringdon: Old Buildings in London Street

Above: An Edwardian view of London Street, looking eastwards towards Folly Hill around 1912. *Below*: a recent photograph, taken from the same vantage point. The three-storey brick building that can be seen in the distance is The Laurels, an early nineteenth-century town house. The Firs, to its left, is a slightly earlier Georgian house, while the gabled building that can be discerned in the distance is the former Female School of Industry, an institution that provided for the needs of pauper children.

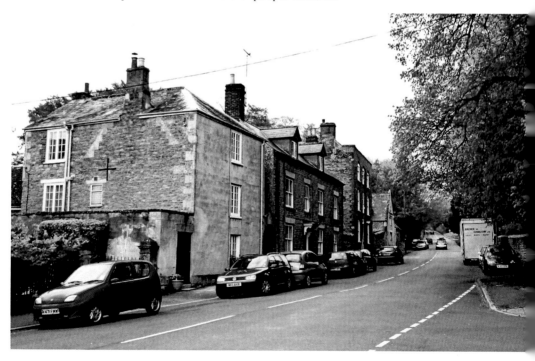

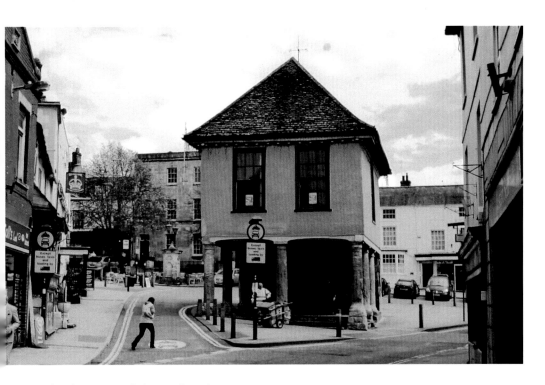

Faringdon: Around the Market Place

Above: A view of the Town Hall and Market Place, photographed from the Cornmarket. *Below*: A general view, looking northwards from the Market Place, with the Crown Hotel visible to the left. The Crown, now known as The Old Crown Coaching Inn, dates from the seventeenth century, although the frontage was remodelled during the following century. Portwell House, to the right of the present-day Crown, may once have been part of the same property.

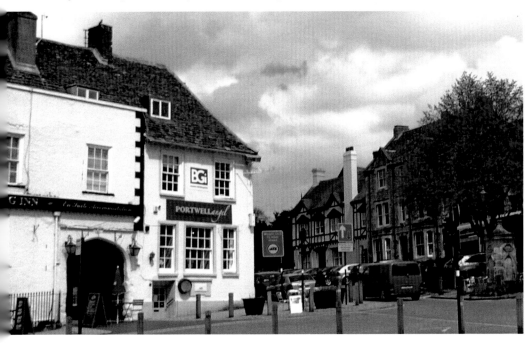

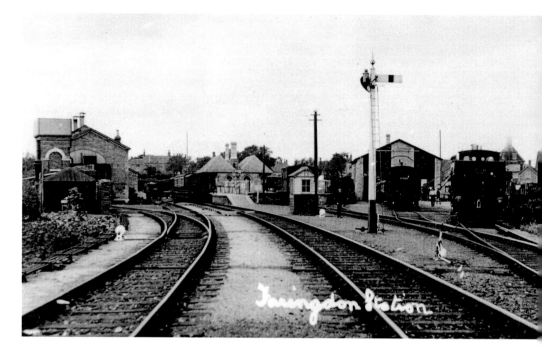

Faringdon: The Faringdon Railway

The Faringdon Railway ran from Faringdon to Uffington Junction, on the GWR main line, a distance of 3½ miles. The railway was authorised in 1860 and opened on 1 June 1864. Faringdon station boasted an interesting station building that had probably been designed by Malachi Bartlett (1802–75) of Witney, a local builder who, in 1863, had been awarded a contract for 'erecting the new station and goods shed at Faringdon'. The upper picture shows the station around 1912, while the lower view dates from the 1960s.

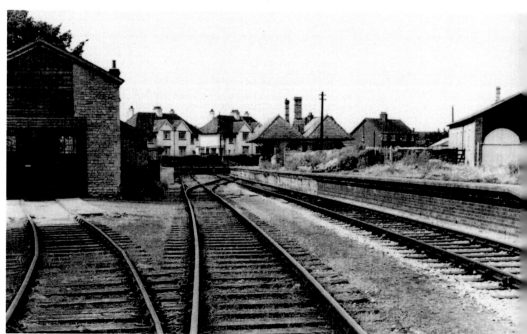

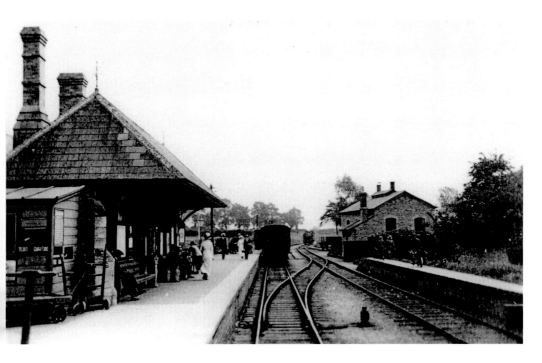

Faringdon: The Faringdon Railway

Sadly, the railway was closed to passengers on Saturday 29 December 1951, although goods traffic was carried until July 1963. The upper view, from an Edwardian postcard, is looking south towards Uffington Junction during the early years of the twentieth century. The lower photograph, which was taken from the same vantage point, provides a glimpse of the distinctive station building during the period of freight-only operation around 1962. The engine shed can be seen to the right in both views.

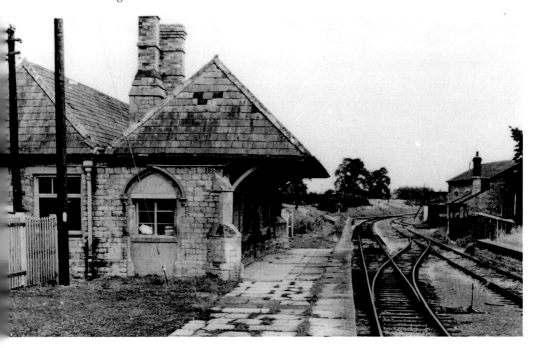

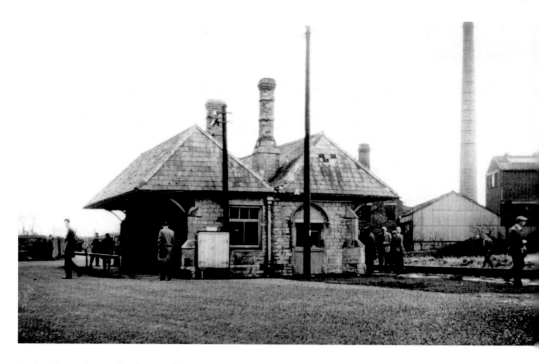

Faringdon: The Faringdon Railway

A rear view of the station building on Sunday 26 April 1959. A party of railway enthusiasts had just arrived in a special excursion train, which was hauled along the branch from Uffington Junction by 13XX class saddle tank No. 1365. The site of the station has now been redeveloped, but the station building has survived more or less intact, as shown in this recent view, which was taken in May 2013.

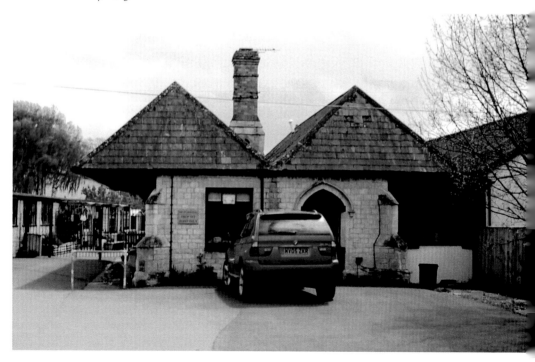

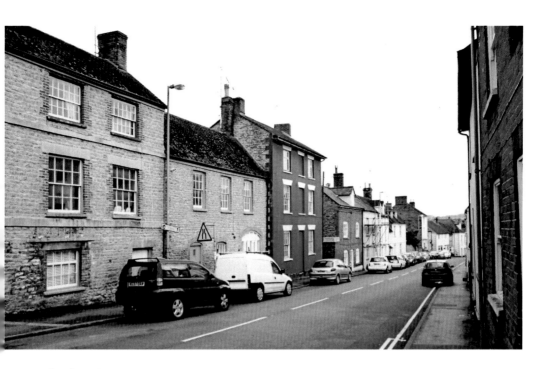

Faringdon: Street Scenes

Two additional views of Faringdon: the upper view showing a group of old buildings on the south side of London Road, while the lower picture provides a final glimpse of the Town Hall, photographed from the east side of the Market Place. The ornate pillar that can be seen to the left is the 'Portwell' pump, which was given to the town in the sixteenth century by Sir Henry Unton for use as a public water supply. The well-head is Victorian.

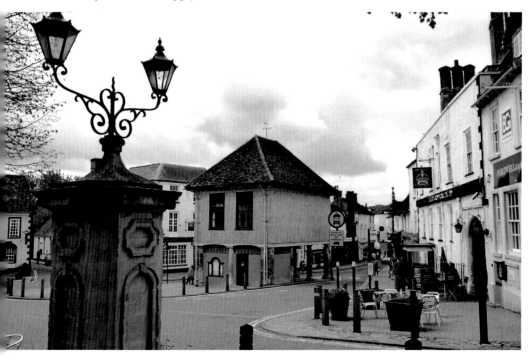

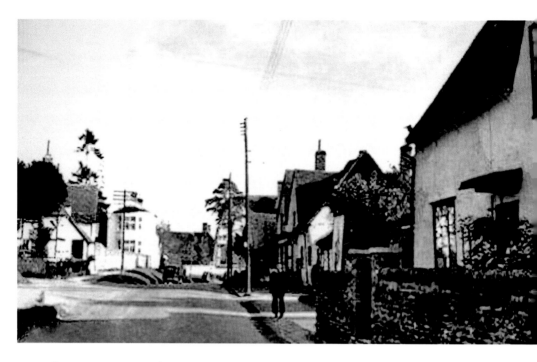

Harwell

Harwell, a large village about 2 miles to the west of Didcot, has long been famous for its fruit orchards. Harwell aerodrome was opened in 1937, and in June 1944 it played a major role in the D-Day invasion of Europe, being one of the airfields used by the glider troops of the 6th Airborne Division. In post-war years, the airfield became the site of the Atomic Energy Research Establishment. The photographs show Harwell High Street around 1925 and in July 2013.

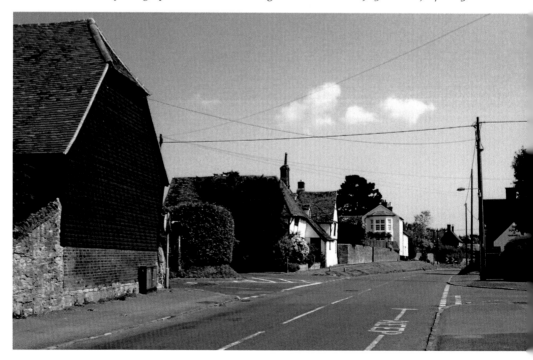

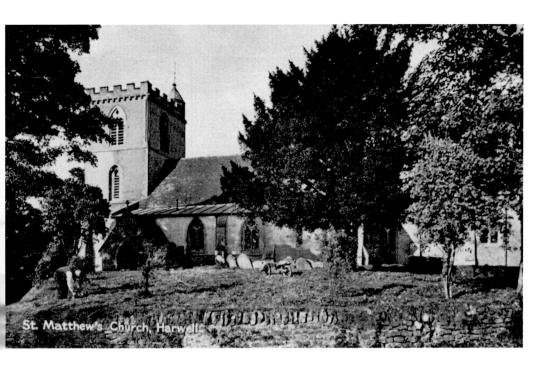

St. Matthew's Church, Harwell

Harwell: St Matthew's Church

The parish church is a cruciform structure with Early English features that date mainly from the thirteenth century, although the chancel was added during the Decorated Period around 1320. The north and south aisles, and the west tower, are of thirteenth-century origin. The interior of the church features some interesting carvings, including the figure of a sleeping man with a bottle, which can be seen near the priest's doorway. The sepia view is from an old postcard, while the colour photograph was taken in July 2013.

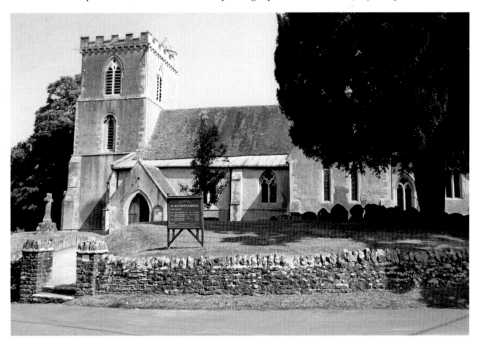

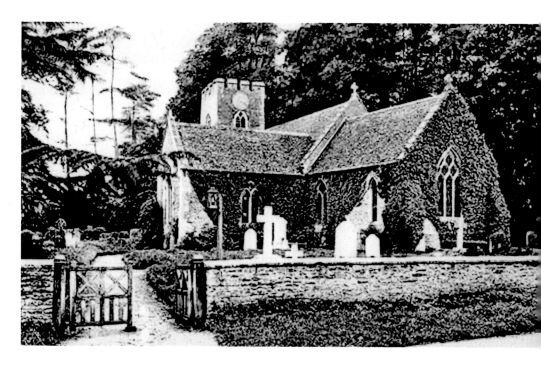

Hinton Waldrist: St Margaret's Church

Hinton Waldrist, about 6 miles to the north-east of Faringdon and about half a mile south of the Thames, sits upon a low plateau, about 200 feet above mean sea level, with attractive views on all sides. The parish church is a cruciform structure with a west tower. The earliest features date back to the mid-thirteenth century, although the building was extensively restored during the Victorian period. The upper view is from an early twentieth-century postcard, whereas the colour photograph was taken in May 2013.

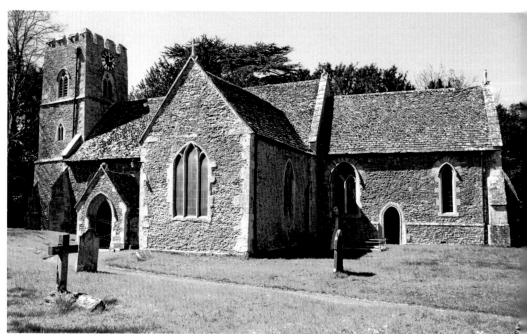

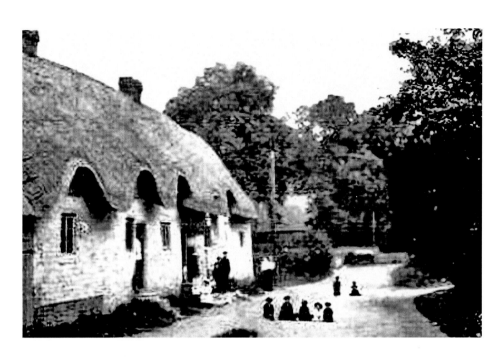

Kingston Little & The Blowing Stone

Above: Kingston Lisle is one of the spring-line villages sited at the foot of the Berkshire Downs along the B4507 road between Wantage and Ashbury. This Edwardian postcard view shows a row of typical old cottages in the village. *Below*: The blowing stone, which can be seen in a cottage garden near the village, is a perforated sarsen that is said to have been used as a horn by King Alfred to summon his army in the event of a Viking attack!

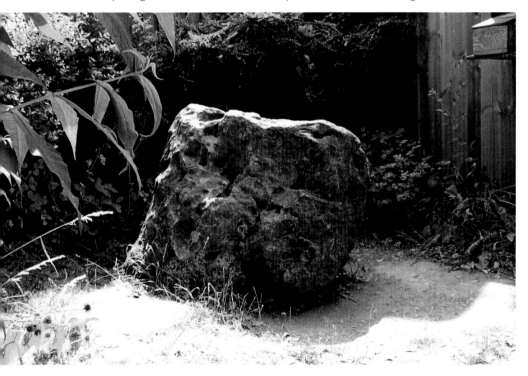

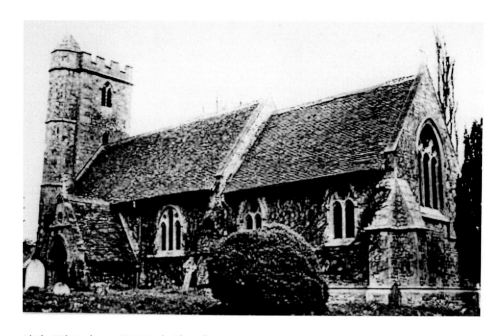

Little Wittenham: St Peter's Church

Little Wittenham is a small village sited near the River Thames, in the shadow of Wittenham Clumps (*see page 25*), about 5 miles south-east of Abingdon. The parish church, comprising a nave, chancel, porch and west tower, was substantially rebuilt by Charles Buckeridge in 1863. The tower features a prominent stair-turret, which seems slightly out of proportion to the main tower – Frederick Brabant described it as 'a strange belfry tower' in the 1911 *Little Guide to Berkshire*.

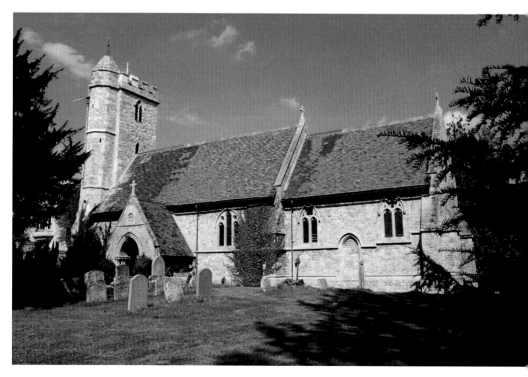

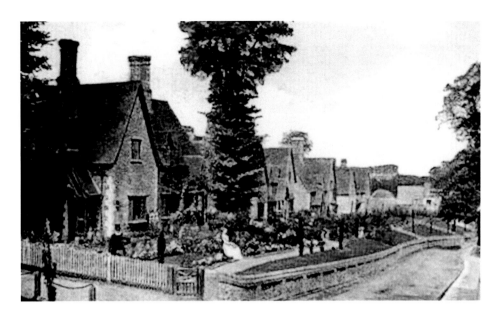

Lockinge

As mentioned on page 14, Robert Lindsay (who was made Lord Wantage in 1885) acquired the Lockinge estate through his marriage to Harriet Lloyd in 1858, and in the ensuing decades he became an archetypal 'improving landlord', with an unshakable faith in material progress. He employed the most advanced methods of cultivation and management, paying particular attention to the villages of Ardington and Lockinge. These two views depict typical estate houses in East Lockinge; the upper view is from an Edwardian colour-tinted postcard.

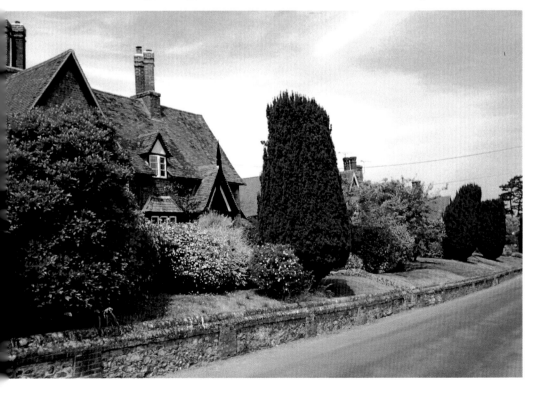

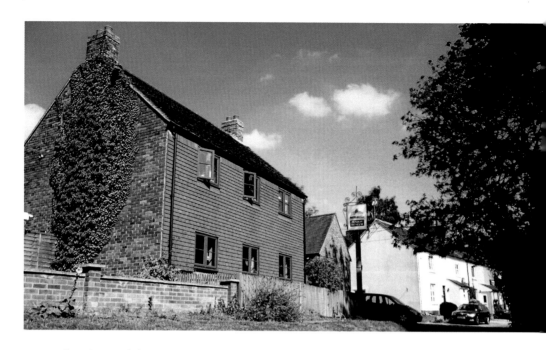

Long Wittenham: High Street & Pendon Museum

Above: In May 1925, a young Australian named Roye England (1906–95) arrived in England, and having 'discovered' the Vale of the White Horse, he became fascinated by its history and historic buildings – many of which were under threat of demolition. Determined to record what was being destroyed, he opened a Youth Hostel at No. 33 High Street, Long Wittenham (formerly The Three Poplars public house) and established a museum of miniature landscape and transport in the garden! *Below*: Pendon's first museum building was an old wooden RAF hut, but the museum now occupies these modern premises at the rear of No. 33 High Street. *Inset*: A general view of Long Wittenham, around 1912.

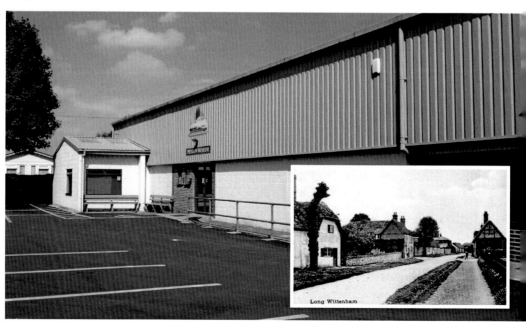

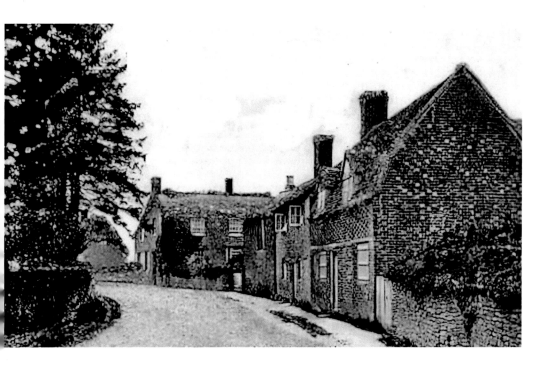

Longworth: Old Buildings in Church Lane

Longworth, a secluded village to the east of Faringdon, is associated with the Victorian novelist Richard Doddridge Blackmore (1825–1900), the author of *Lorna Doone*, who was born in the Vicarage as the third son of the Revd John Blackmore. The village occupies a low plateau of coral rag, affording good views towards the north. The upper view depicts a group of old houses and cottages in Church Lane, probably around 1912, and the recent photograph shows the same buildings in 2013.

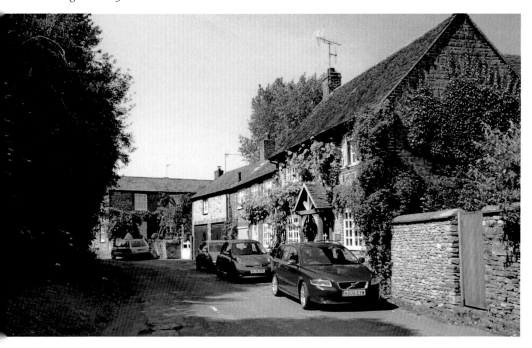

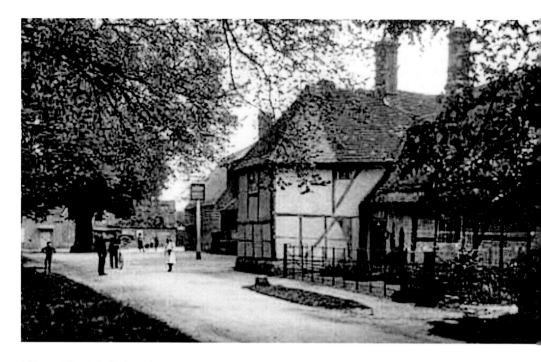

Milton: The Admiral Benbow

Milton is a small village about 3½ miles to the north of Didcot. Although the area is now dominated by the sprawling Milton Park Trading Estate, the village has retained much of its rural character. The upper view depicts the Admiral Benbow pub during the early years of the twentieth century, and the recent colour photograph shows the same building in September 2013. At the time of writing, the property is up for sale.

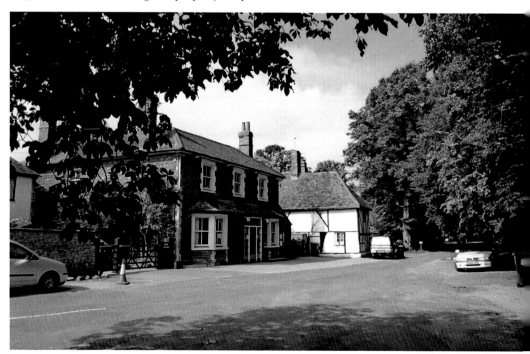

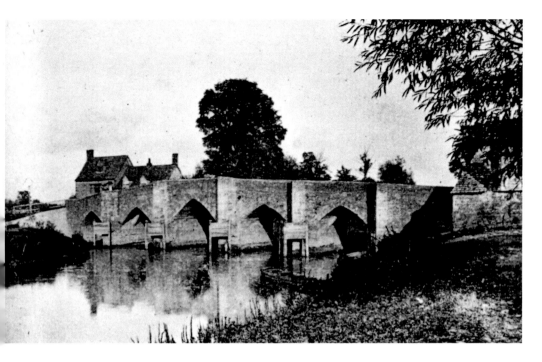

Newbridge

The medieval bridge at Newbridge, 14 miles 61 chains from Oxford, is one of the oldest bridges on the Thames. It has six pointed arches, and dates from the fourteenth century. There are two pubs at Newbridge: the Rose Revived on the north bank and the Maybush Inn sited on the south side of the river. The upper view shows the ancient bridge around 1910, while the colour view was taken from a similar vantage point on the south bank in May 2013.

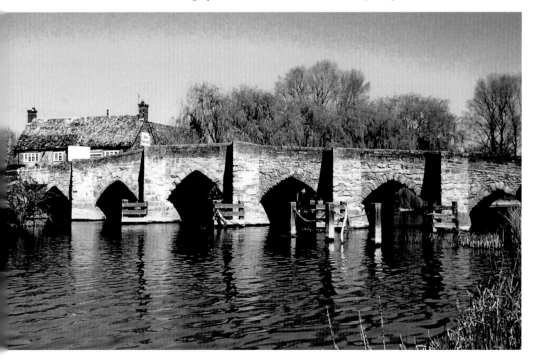

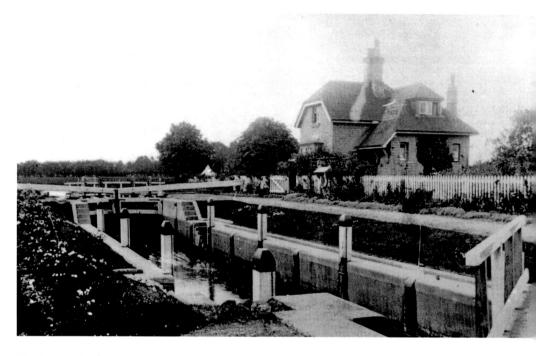

Northmoor Lock

Northmoor Lock, 12 miles 47 chains upstream from Oxford, was opened in 1896. The sepia view provides a glimpse of the lock chamber and lock-keeper's cottage from the east around 1912, whereas the colour photograph is looking in the opposite direction towards Oxford in July 2013. The dimensions of the lock are 113½ feet by 15 feet. At the time of writing, there are proposals to replace the old weir with a fully mechanised weir.

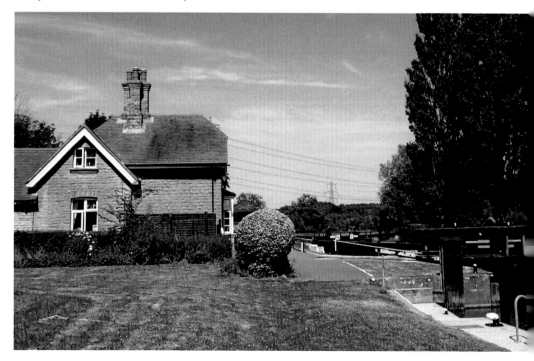

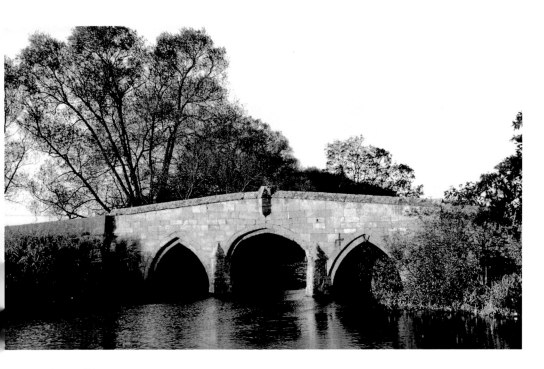

Radcot Bridge

Above: Dating back to the thirteenth century, the triple-arched Radcot Bridge, 24 miles 74 chains upstream from Oxford, is one of the oldest bridges on the Thames. However, in 1787 this old bridge was bypassed by a new cut, which is spanned by a single-arched bridge; there are thus two river bridges at this point, together with a millstream channel. *Below*: The Swan Hotel is situated immediately to the north of the New Cut.

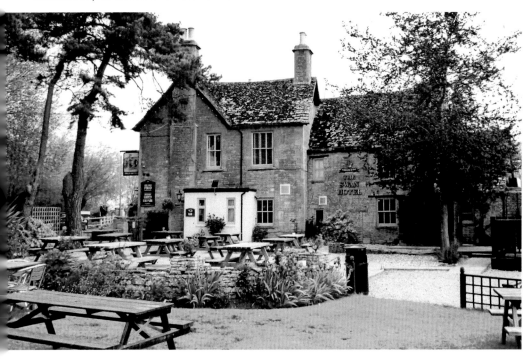

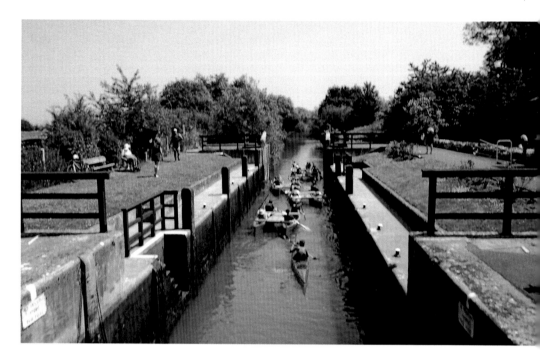

Rushey Lock & Weir

Situated 21 miles 50 chains upstream from Oxford, Rushey Lock was opened in 1790 and rebuilt in 1898. The upper picture is looking east towards Oxford in July 2013, while the sepia photograph, which was taken about ninety years earlier, shows the lock-keeper's house and the adjacent Rushey Weir. The lock chamber has a length of 113½ feet and a width of 15 feet. This stretch of the river is particularly remote, with few signs of habitation in the immediate vicinity.

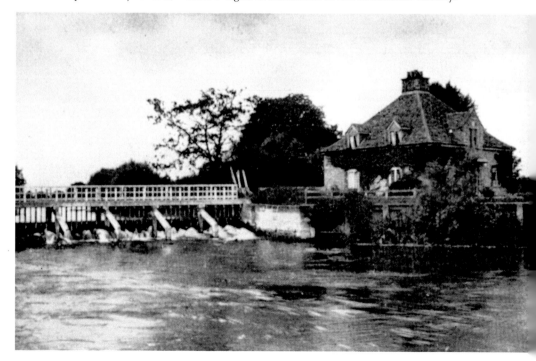

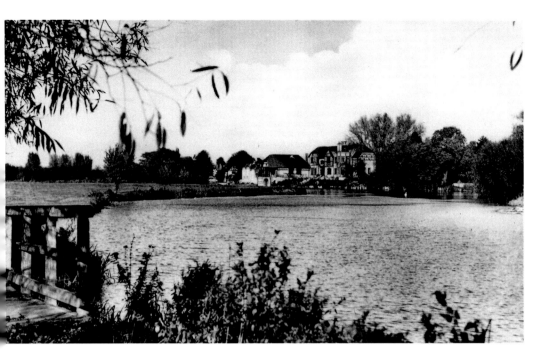

Shillingford Bridge

Above: Although the village of Shillingford is situated on the north, or Oxfordshire, side of the Thames, the Shillingford Bridge Hotel is on the former Berkshire bank at the south end of Shillingford Bridge. The postcard view of around 1950 is looking northwards across the River Thames to a large house known as Shillingford Court, which was erected in 1895–97 for Frederick Mortimer, who sometimes entertained the Prince of Wales as a house guest. *Below:* The colour photograph shows a typical stretch of the river in 2013.

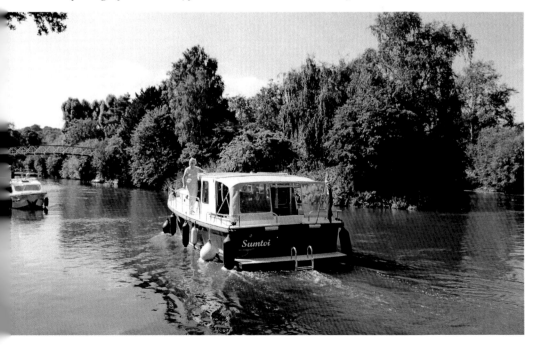

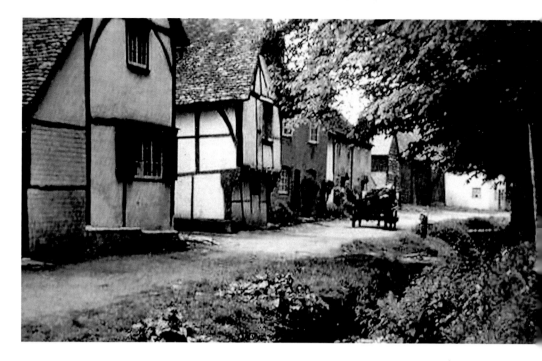

Steventon: The Causeway – The Old Vicarage

Steventon, a large village sited around 4 miles to the west of Didcot, extends from north to south along the B4017 road, known as the High Street, and from north-east to south-west alongside an ancient raised flood-path known as the Causeway, which is said to have been constructed by the monks of an alien priory belonging to the Abbey of Bec, in Normandy. The upper view shows timber-framed buildings beside the Causeway around 1912, while the colour photograph was taken from a similar position in July 2013.

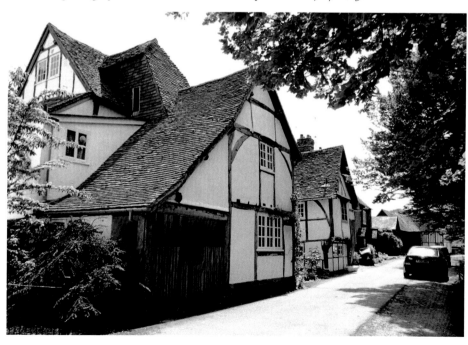

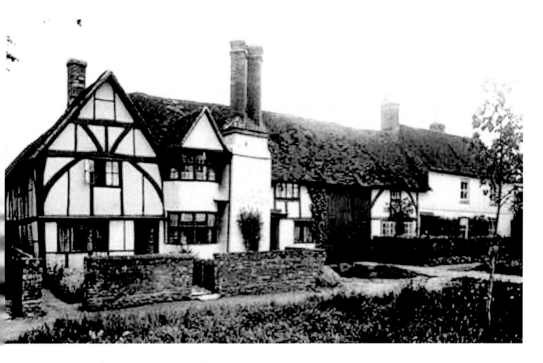

Steventon: The Causeway – Godfrey's Cottage

There are, in all, about half a dozen large timber-framed houses along the tree-lined Causeway, one of which is Godfrey's Cottage, No. 77, which is shown in the upper picture. This picturesque structure, which is probably of Tudor origin, has a cross-wing at its eastern end, together with a large, stone chimney stack surmounted by diagonal brick chimneys; a large gateway to the west of the chimney gave access to agricultural buildings at the rear. The lower picture shows a neighbouring property known as the Priory.

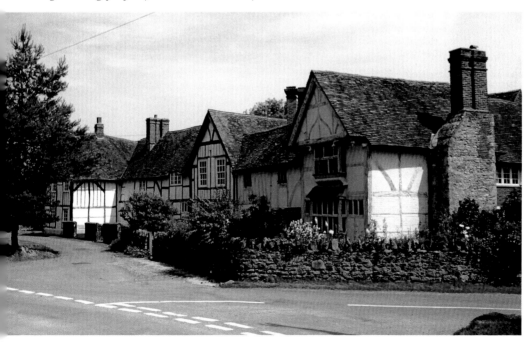

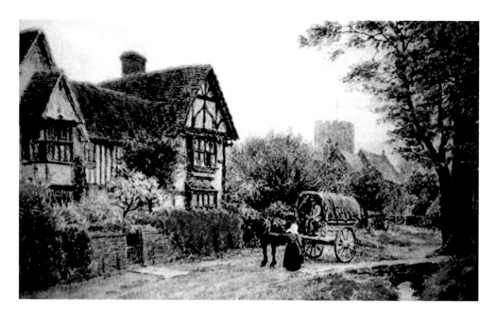

Steventon: The Causeway – Priory Cottages

Above: This Edwardian colour-tinted postcard provides a slightly idealised impression of the Priory, which is situated beyond the level crossing at the western extremity of the Causeway. Parts of this quaint old structure date back to the fourteenth century. *Below*: A recent view, showing Priory Cottages from a position slightly further to the east in July 2013. The raised Causeway is visible to the right of the picture; most of these old houses have been sub-divided into smaller properties.

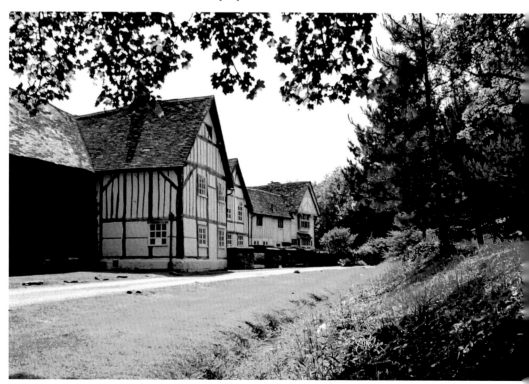

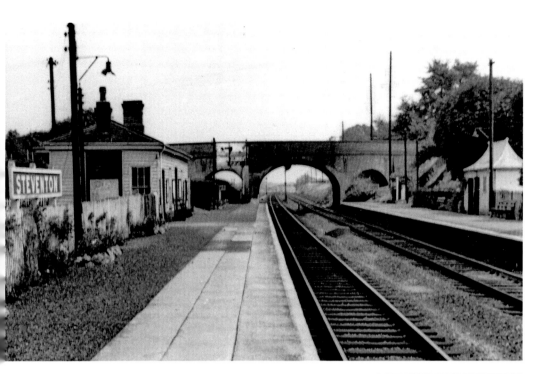

Steventon: The Railway Station

Steventon was served by a station on the Great Western Railway main line, which was opened on 1 June 1840. The station was situated at the eastern extremity of the village, and it consisted of up and down platforms for passenger traffic, together with a small goods yard. The upper picture shows the station in the 1960s, looking east towards Paddington.

Steventon station was closed to passengers on Saturday 5 December 1964, although goods traffic was handled until the following March. The station building and platforms were subsequently demolished, but two stone-built railway houses have nevertheless survived in the former station yard, and one of these is shown in the lower picture. This substantial, Brunel-designed stone-built structure was constructed to accommodate the Superintendent of the Line, and it was also used for GWR board meetings in the early days of the company.

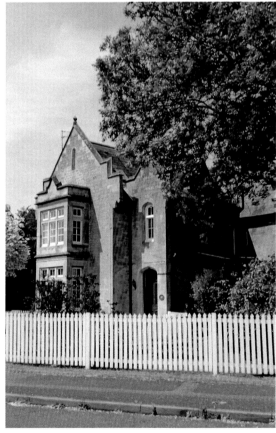

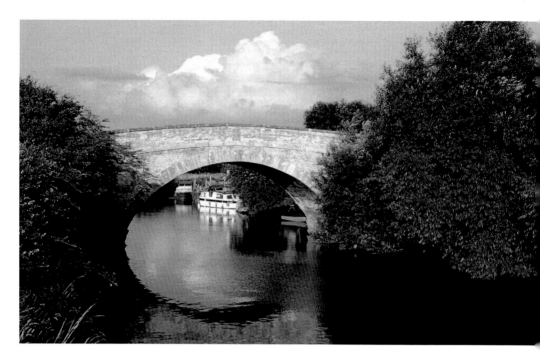

Tadpole Bridge & the Trout Inn

Tadpole Bridge, 20 miles 73 chains from Oxford, was built at the end of the eighteenth century on the site of Tadpole Weir, the original bridge being of timber construction. The present bridge, which incorporates a single span of 15 feet, was completed around 1800. The upper view depicts the bridge in 1987, while the more recent photograph shows the Trout Inn, which is on the south bank of the river. There was once a busy wharf here, the most important source of traffic being domestic coal.

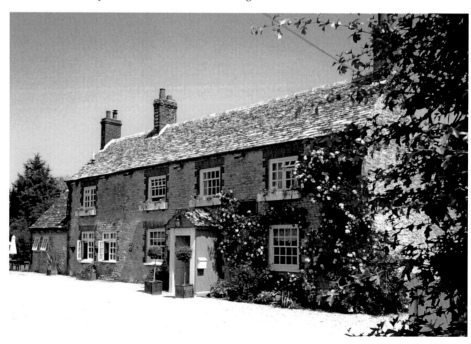

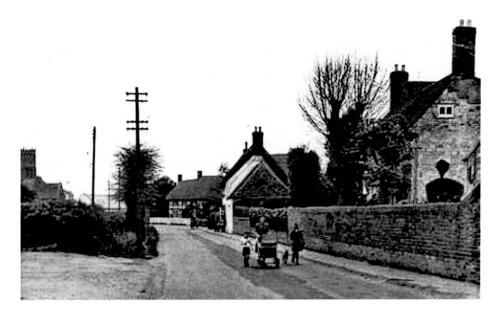

Uffington: Broad Street

Uffington, some 4 miles to the south of Faringdon, is a very attractive village with many interesting old houses and cottages, some of which are built of the local chalk, while others are constructed of an admixture of chalk and brickwork. The upper picture from a 1930s postcard is looking westwards along Broad Street, whereas the recent colour photograph was taken from a vantage point slightly further to the east.

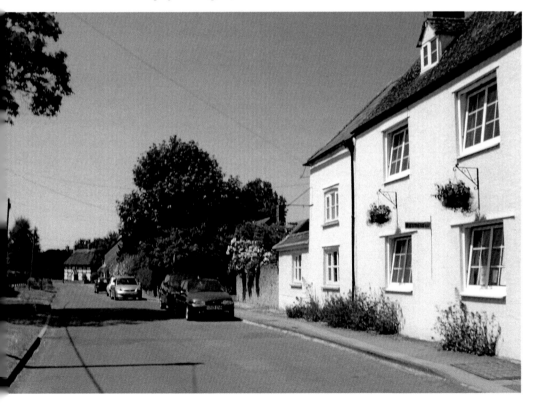

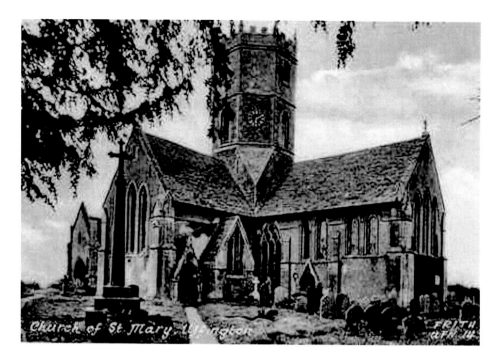

Uffington: St Mary's Church

St Mary's parish church is an impressive, cruciform structure with an unusual octagonal tower. It was built in the thirteenth century, and its architecural details reflect the Early English style. The spire was blown down during a gale in December 1740. The church contains a memorial brass to Thomas Hughes (1822–96), the author of *Tom Brown's Schooldays*, who was born in the village (although he is buried in Brighton). The colour photograph was taken in 2013, while the sepia view is of around 1912.

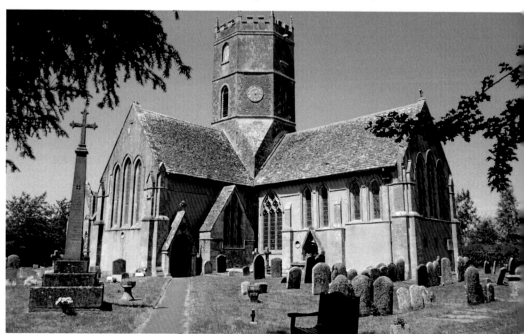

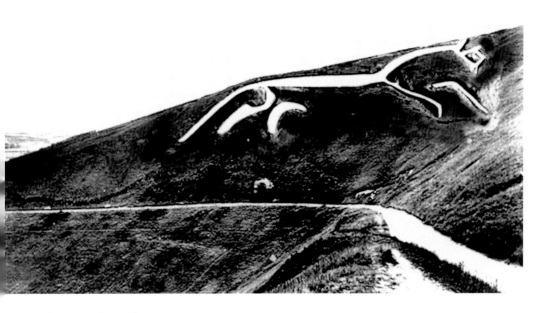

Uffington: The White Horse

White Horse Hill, to the south of Uffington, is the site of a complex of prehistoric earthworks, including Uffington Castle and Dragon Hill, as well as the famous White Horse. The sepia view, which purports to show the horse from Dragon Hill Road, has probably been retouched, as the ancient hill-carving is only visible from a distance (or from the air). The lower view is looking northwards across the Vale, with the White Horse partially visible in the foreground.

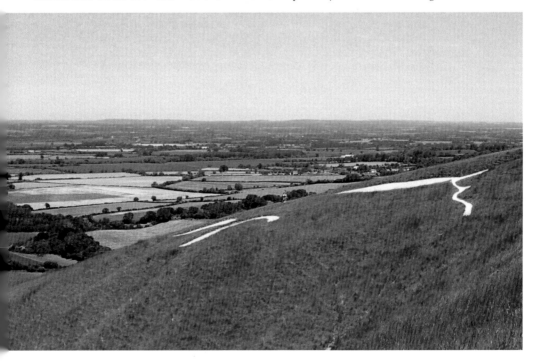

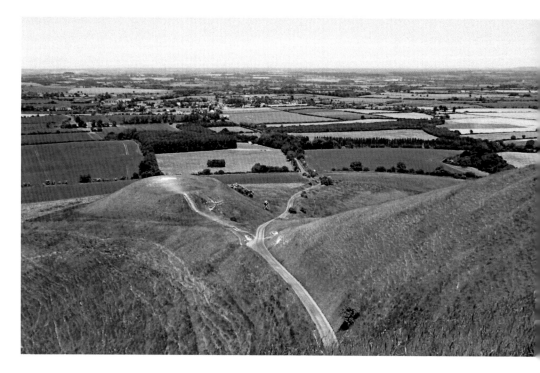

Uffington Dragon Hill and Tom Brown's School Museum

Above: According to tradition, Dragon Hill, below the White Horse, is the place where St George slew the dragon. The mysterious patch of bare chalk on top of the hill marks the spot where the dragon's blood was spilled! *Below*: This chalk building near the church is dated 1617, and was used as a village school for many years. It features in *Tom Brown's Schooldays* and now serves as a local history museum.

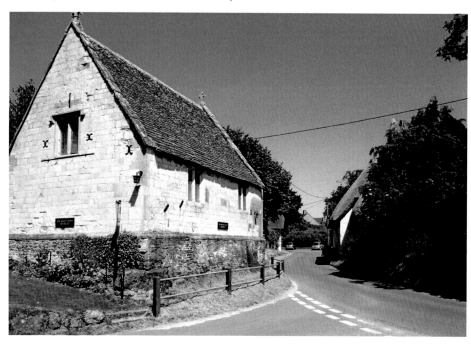

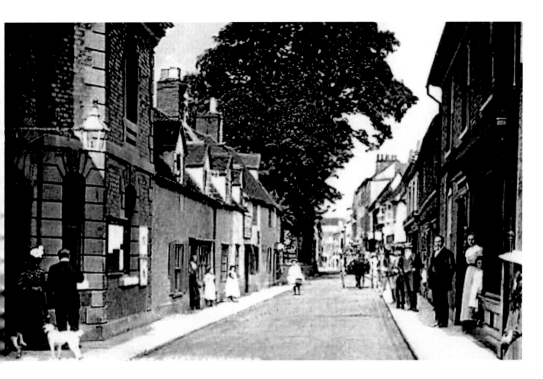

Wallingford: St Mary's Street

Wallingford was one of the fortified burghs that protected Wessex against the Danes, but this did not prevent it from being burned by the Vikings in 1006. Although it is situated beyond the confines of the Vale of the White Horse, it was one of the towns transferred from Berkshire to Oxfordshire in 1974 and, as such, it deserves at least some consideration here. These Edwardian postcard views show St Mary's Street and Wallingford Bridge during the early years of the twentieth century.

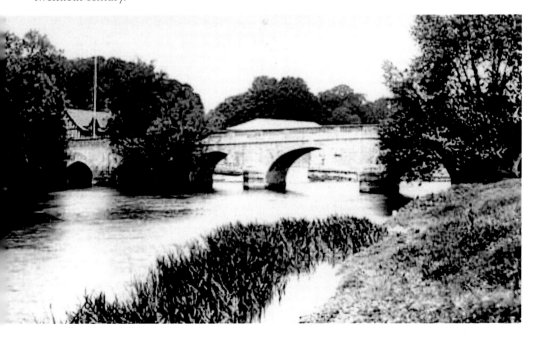

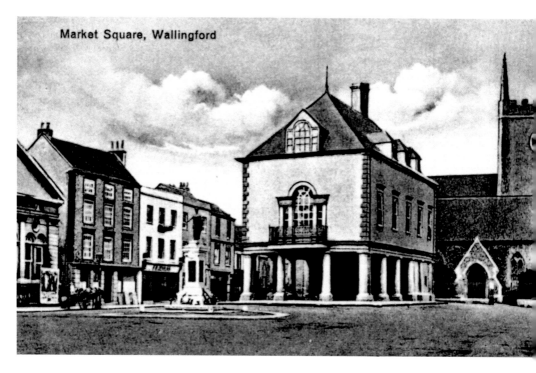

Market Square, Wallingford

Wallingford: The Town Hall & Market Place

The upper view, taken from an Edwardian postcard, shows the Market Place and the seventeenth-century town hall, which stands upon Doric columns and incorporates an open loggia. This handsome building was altered in the nineteenth century, and again in the 1930s. The recent colour photograph, taken in September 2013, shows the building from a different angle.

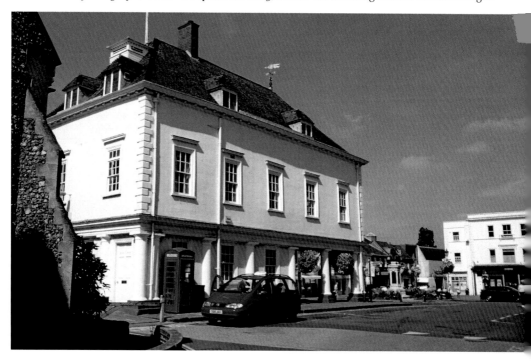

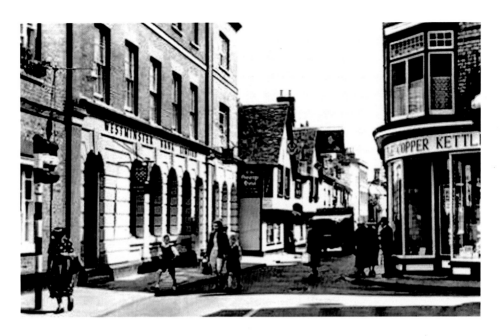

Wallingford: The High Street

The upper view is looking east along the High Street, probably around 1950, while the lower photograph shows a similar scene in September 2013. This part of the street is dominated by two three-storey buildings: the former Lamb Inn (now a shopping arcade) and the neighbouring National Westminster bank. The bank was originally an eighteenth-century town house, whereas the Lamb is somewhat older, and dates from the seventeenth century, although its main façade was reconstructed during the Georgian period.

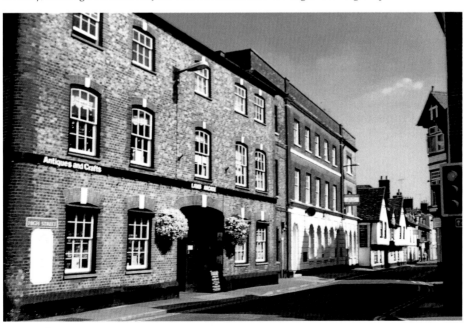

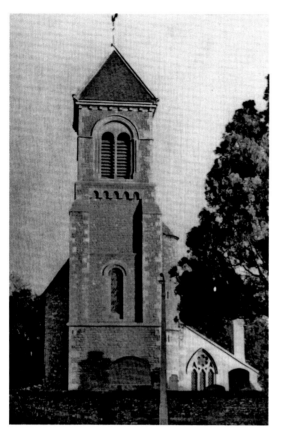

Wallingford: St Leonard's Church
It is said that Wallingford once had no fewer than eleven churches, but only three now remain. Of these, St Leonard's is perhaps the most interesting. This Norman church was damaged in the Civil War and rebuilt in 1704, while in 1849 the building was extensively reconstructed by A. W. Hakewill. In its present form, the church incorporates a nave, south aisle, chancel and a west tower, the oldest parts being the nave and chancel, whereas the tower, apse and nave arcade are of Victorian origin. The upper view is from a postcard of around 1930, while the lower picture shows the south side of the church in September 2013. The churchyard is now a nature reserve.

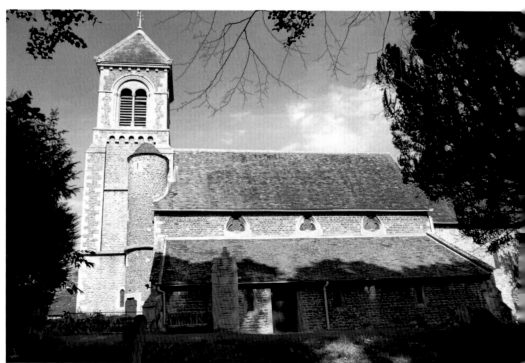

Wallingford: St Leonard's Church

Right: An interior view of St Leonard's church, looking east towards the altar, and showing the Norman chancel arch, which is adorned with elaborate diaper-work. A second Norman arch at the end of the chancel gives access to the remodelled apse. It is thought that these Romanseque arches date from around 1150. *Below:* This final view of Wallingford is looking northwards along St Mary's Street, with the Coach Makers Arms featuring prominently to the left of the picture.

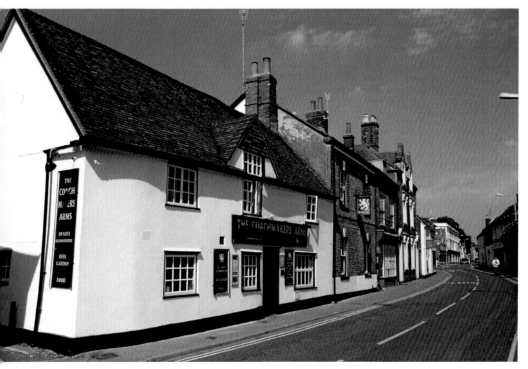

Interior, St. Leonard's Church, Wallingford

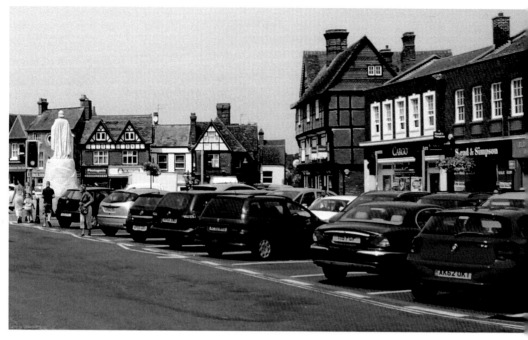

Wantage: Origins of the Town

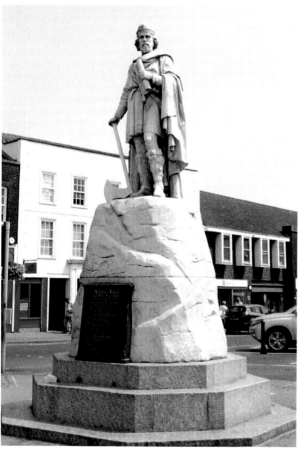

Situated at the foot of the Berkshire Downs, Wantage is associated with Alfred the Great who, according to Asser, the King's biographer, was born in 849 'at the Royal Estate called Wantage, in the district known as Berkshire'. As a royal manor, Wantage was obviously a place of considerable importance during the Anglo-Saxon period, although in later years it developed along more modest lines as a typical market town, catering for the needs of the surrounding district.

The manor of Wantage was granted to Fulk Fitzwarren during the reign of King John, while the neighbouring manor of Priorshold was granted to the Abbot of Bec. Although these medieval landlords were absentees, the topography of the town, with its compact Market Place, hints at a policy of deliberate town-planning during the Middle Ages. The accompanying photographs show the Market Place, which is graced by a fine statue of King Alfred.

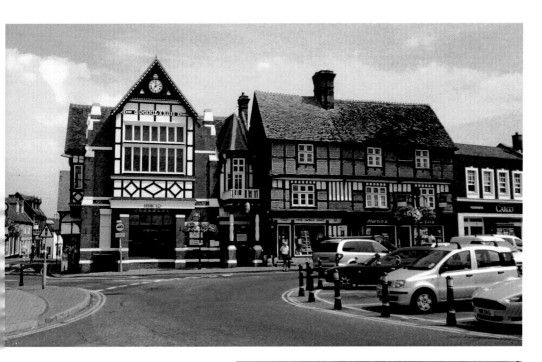

Wantage: King Alfred's Statue

Above: Many of the town's older buildings are constructed of local red and grey brickwork, as exemplified by the HSBC Bank and two neighbouring shops in the north-western corner of the Market Place, the shops at Nos 39 and 40 being seventeenth-century timber-framed structures with decorative herringbone brick panels.

Right: The sepia photograph is a detailed study of King Alfred's statue, which was carved out of white Sicilian marble by the eminent German-born sculptor Count Victor Gleichen (1833–91). The statue, depicting Alfred as a warrior and law-giver, was presented to the town by Lord Wantage, and unveiled by the Prince of Wales on Saturday 14 July 1877, the day being treated as a public holiday in Wantage and the surrounding district. Count Gleichen, who had served in the British Navy during the Crimean War, was the Queen's cousin, and a personal friend of Lord Wantage.

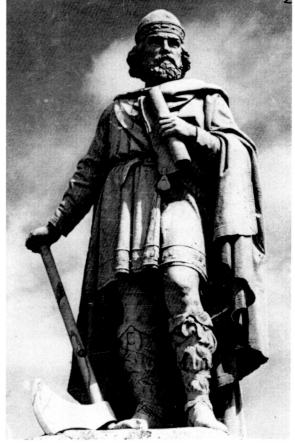

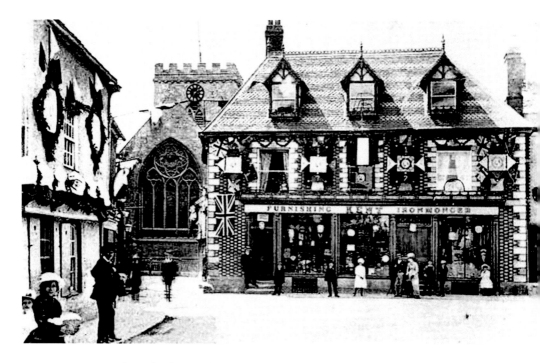

Wantage: Ornate Shops in the Market Place

This ornate building at the west end of the Market Place is dated 1708, but its present appearance is entirely Victorian in character, the street frontage having been remodelled during the late nineteenth century. The building is of red-brick construction, with limestone dressings and a steeply pitched hipped roof. The dormer windows have miniature balconies, while the roofline is adorned with crested ridge tiles. The sepia postcard view dates from around 1912, while the colour photograph was taken in July 2013.

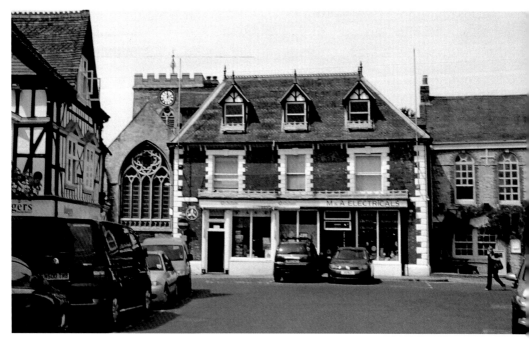

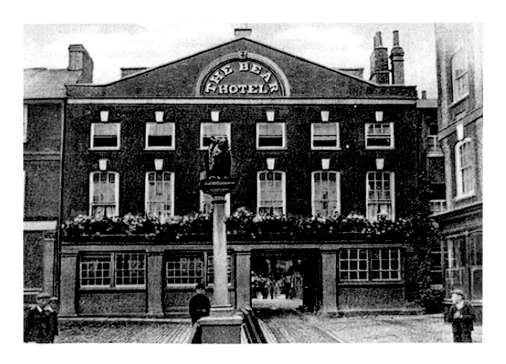

Wantage: The Bear Hotel

The Bear Hotel, on the south side of the Market Place, is a seventeenth-century structure that was remodelled during the early Georgian period. It is of red-brick construction with a symmetrical façade and a moulded cornice, which is surmounted by a pediment. The name of the inn is prominently displayed in a half-lunette. The upper view shows the hotel during the early years of the twentieth century, and the colour photograph was taken in July 2013.

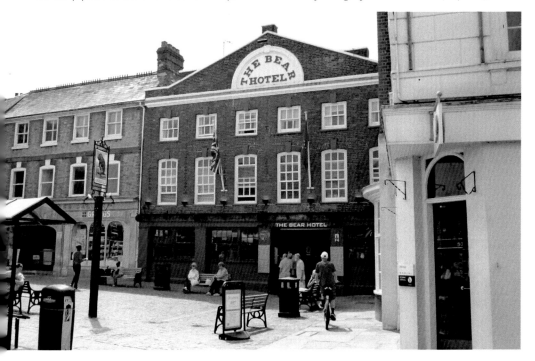

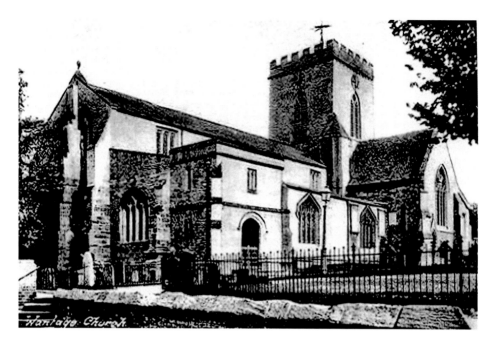

Wantage: The Church of St Peter & St Paul

The parish church is a large cruciform building, incorporating a nave, aisles, transepts, chancel and a central tower, together with a south porch and chapels to the east of both transepts. The church was extensively restored in the 1850s by the Victorian architect George Edmund Street (1824–81), while in 1877 the nave and aisles were extended westwards by William Butterfield (1814–1900), who also moved the south porch to the west end of the building. The photographs were taken around 1912 and in 2013.

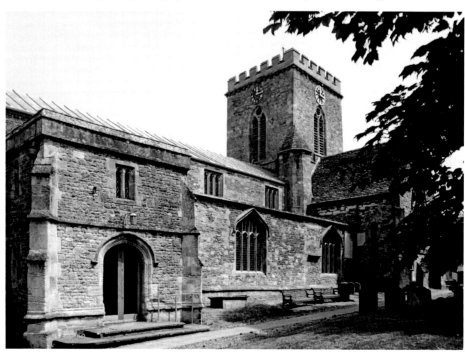

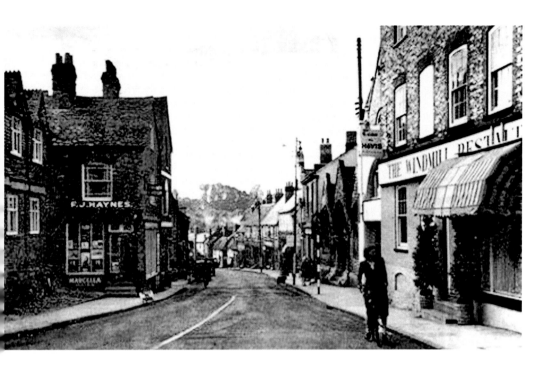

Wantage: Mill Street Looking Westwards

Mill Street, which runs more or less due westwards from the Market Place, drops fairly steeply towards the Letcombe Brook. It contains a mixture of houses and commercial properties, as shown in the accompanying pictures, the upper view dating from around 1950, whereas the recent colour photograph was taken in July 2013. The building on the extreme right (Nos 2 and 4), now a restaurant, is a grey-brick Georgian house with contrasting red-brick quoins and dressings.

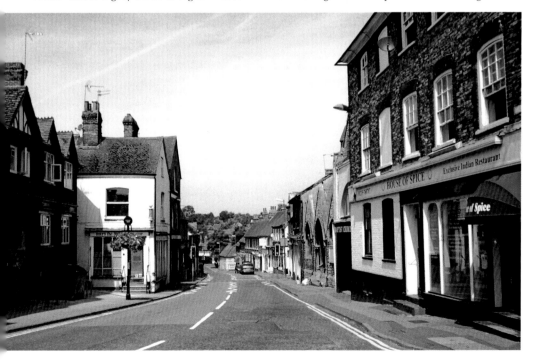

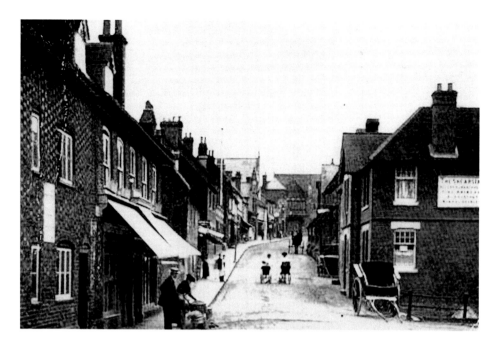

Wantage: Mill Street Looking Eastwards

This Edwardian tinted postcard view is looking uphill in the opposite direction, from the bottom of Mill Street towards the Market Place. The recent photograph, taken in 2013, was taken from a position slightly further to the east. No. 20, the Georgian town house that can be seen to the left of the picture, is of grey-brick construction with red-brick quoins and a gabled roof. The building with the high roof that is visible in the distance is Wantage Baptist chapel.

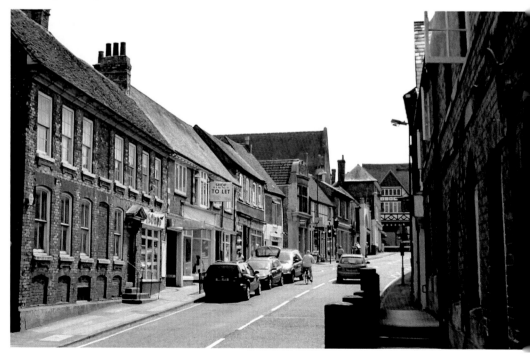

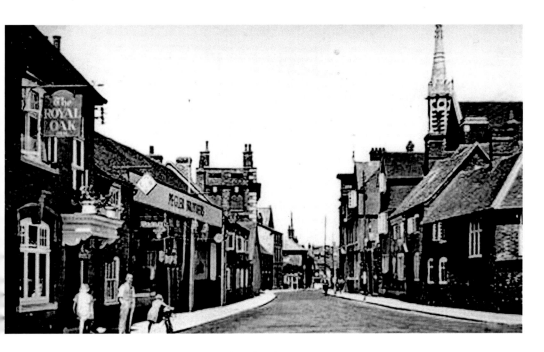

Wantage: Newbury Street & St Mary's School

Newbury Street, now part of the busy A338 road, extends southwards from the Market Place. It contains several notable buildings, including the former St Mary's School and chapel, the main school building having been converted from a Georgian town house, while the adjoining red-brick chapel was erected in 1898/89 to a design by Charles Edward Ponting (1849–1932). Its west façade features a crocketed spire that can be seen in the photographs. The chapel is now a dental surgery.

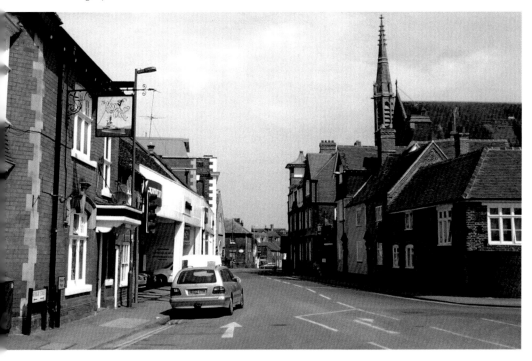

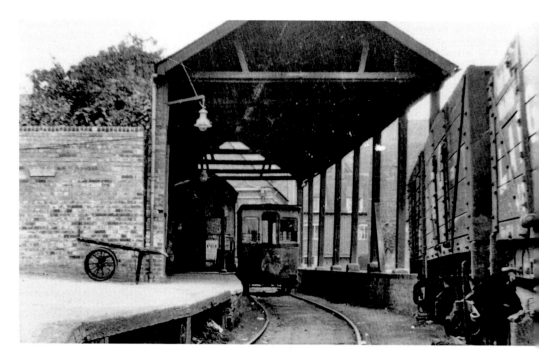

Wantage: The Wantage Tramway – Mill Street Terminus

Wantage was formerly linked to the main line railway network by the Wantage Tramway, which was opened for goods traffic on 1 October 1875 and for the carriage of passengers on 11 October. The tramway commenced in the yard of the GWR station at Wantage Road and, for much of its length, this 2½-mile line was laid alongside the main A338 road. At Wantage, the tramway ended in a small terminus known as Wantage Town station. The upper view shows the passenger platform around 1925, while the recent view shows the still-extant terminal building in 2013.

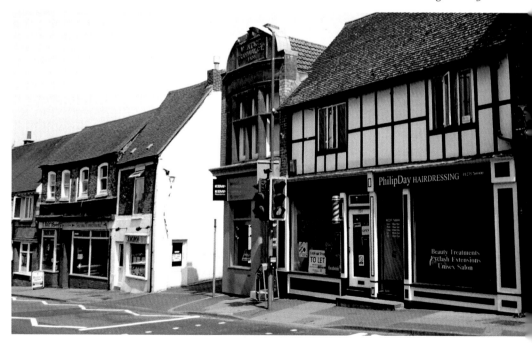

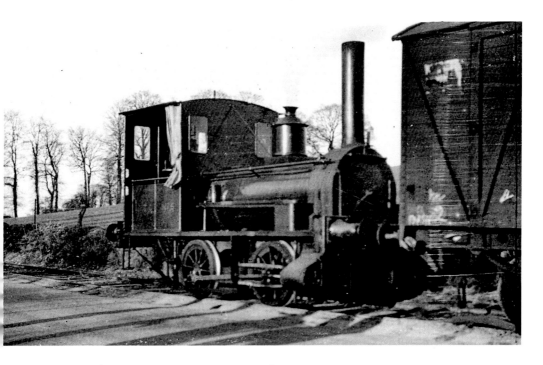

Wantage – The Wantage Tramway – *Jane* **and** *Mary*
Wantage Tramway passenger vehicles were hauled by tram engines with fully enclosed wheels, boilers and motion, but conventional locomotives were employed for hauling freight trains; the longest-serving engines were Nos 5 and 7, known colloquially as *Jane* and *Mary,* which were built in 1857 and 1888 respectively. The upper view shows *Jane* hauling a freight train on the roadside tramway, while the lower view depicts *Mary* with tramcar No. 4 at Grove Bridge, probably around 1912.

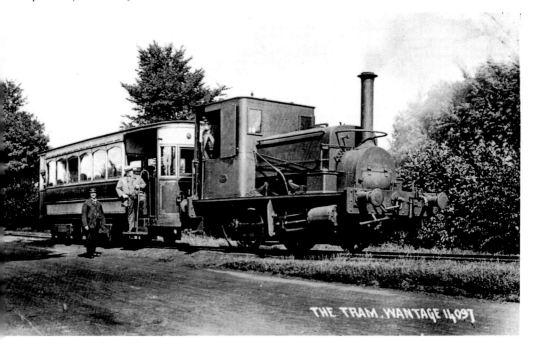

THE TRAM .WANTAGE 14097

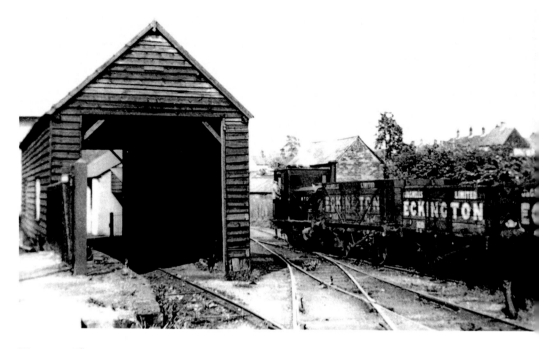

Wantage: The Wantage Tramway – Goods Yards

Above: Engine No. 7 carries out shunting operations in the very cramped goods yard at Wantage Town. The wooden engine shed that can be seen to the left spanned a siding that served Wantage Gasworks. In 1905, the tramway opened an additional goods yard known as the Lower Yard, which was sited at the end of a short goods branch that diverged from the tramway 'main line' at Grove Street Crossing and ended at the bottom of Mill Street. *Below*: Tramcars 3 and 2 at Wantage Town.

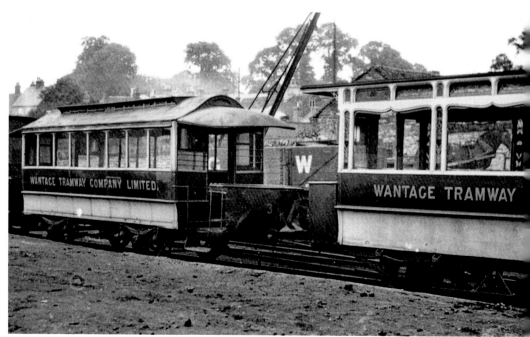

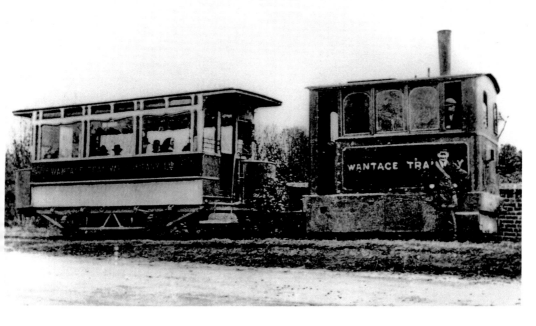

Wantage: The Wantage Tramway – Tram Engine No. 6

These two views of the tramway were taken during the early years of the twentieth century, and they both show WTC tram engine No. 6. This Matthews Patent Tram Engine was sent for trials on the Wantage line in 1882 but, as nobody wanted to buy the locomotive, it remained out-of-use until 1888, when it was finally purchased for employment on the Wantage route. Thereafter, as WTC No. 6, the engine gave many years of useful service. No. 6 was withdrawn in 1925 and scrapped in 1931.

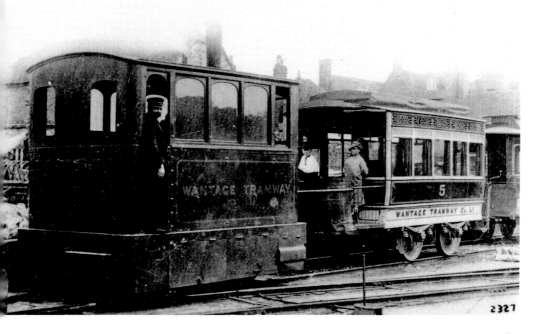

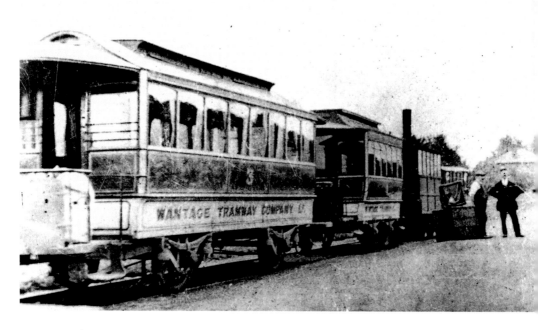

Wantage: The Wantage Tramway – Wantage Road

The upper view shows Tram Engine No. 4 and passenger cars 3 and 1 in Wantage Road goods yard around 1910, while the recent picture, taken from a position slightly further to the south, shows part of the former tramway route at the entrance to the GWR goods yard. Engine No. 4 was purchased in 1877 from Henry Hughes of the Falcon Engine & Car Works, Loughborough. It had 7-inch by 12-inch cylinders and a fully enclosed body; it was scrapped in 1920.

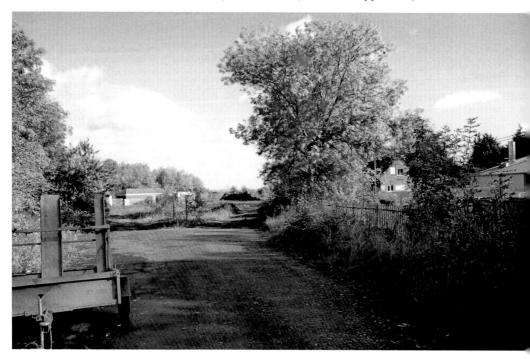

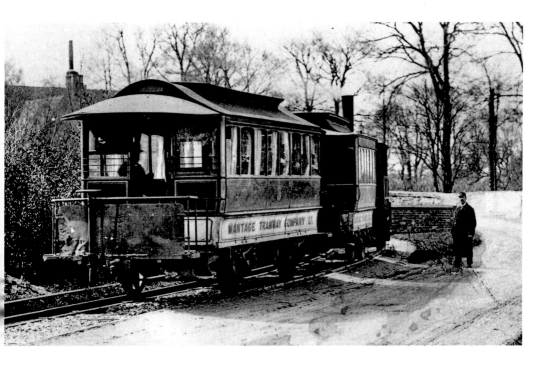

Wantage: The Wantage Tramway – Grove Bridge & the Lower Yard
Above: Tram engine No. 4 pauses at Grove Bridge, while hauling tramcars 3 and 1. Grove Bridge was one of four intermediate halts or stopping places on the roadside tramway between Wantage Road and Wantage Town; it also boasted a short siding for goods traffic. *Below*: The area around the Lower Yard and neighbouring industrial premises has now been redeveloped, and this extensive site is now occupied by shops, cars parks and residential developments.

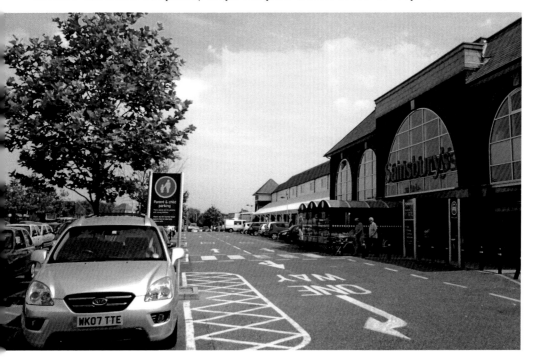

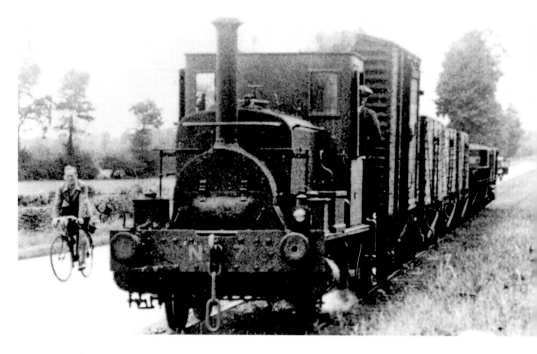

Wantage: The Wantage Tramway – The Final Years

The Wantage Tramway lost its passenger services on 31 July 1925, but freight traffic was carried until December 1945. The upper photograph shows locomotive No. 7 *Mary* with a short freight train alongside the A338 road, while the lower view shows *Mary* hauling No. 5 *Jane* along the tramway for the last time. The latter engine was, for many years, displayed as a static exhibit at Wantage Road station but, happily, this venerable locomotive is now preserved at the Didcot Railway Centre.

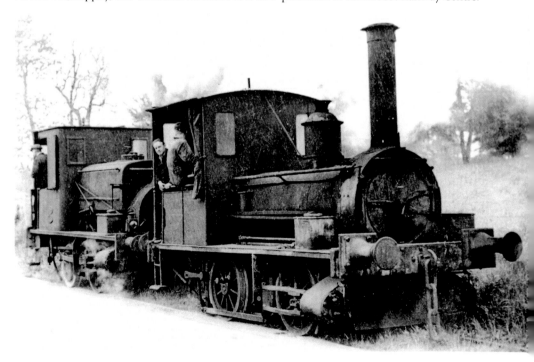

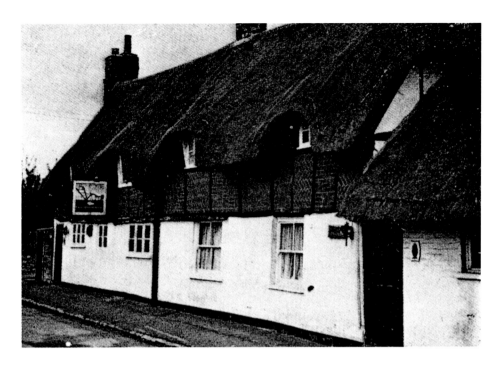

West Hanney: The Plough Inn

West Hanney, about 6 miles to the west of Didcot, is virtually contiguous with East Hanney, the two villages being connected by School Road. The Plough Inn is a seventeenth-century structure with a brick-built ground storey and a timber-framed upper storey, the timber framing being filled by brickwork nogging. The thatched roof boasts upswept 'eyebrow' dormers, the overall effect being particularly picturesque. The upper view dates from around 1950, whereas the colour photograph was taken in July 2013.

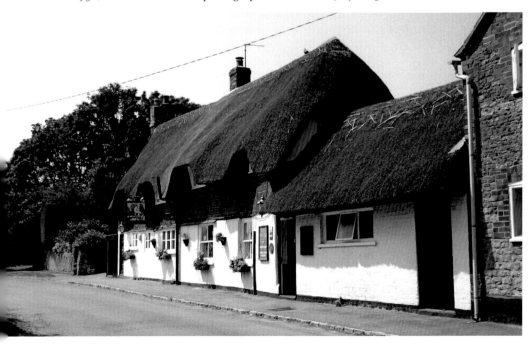

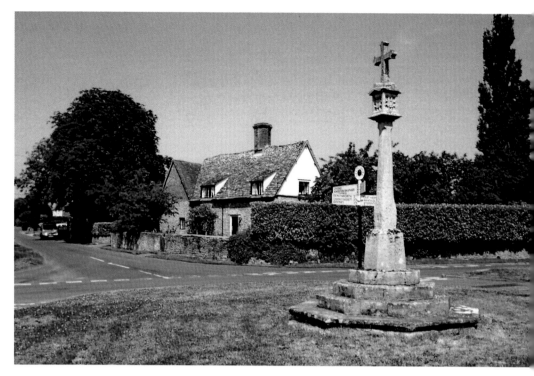

West Hanney: The Cross on the Green

West Hanney has a fairly spacious green, together with a village cross that incorporates a stepped plinth and a tapering shaft. Although this fifteenth-century structure, known as the Butter Cross, was taken down at the time of the Reformation, it was reconstructed in 1908. The colour photograph is looking northwards in July 2013, while the sepia postcard view shows the other side of the cross around 1912.

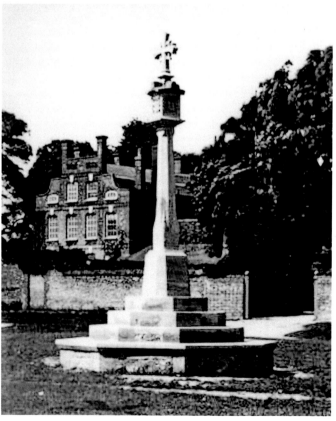

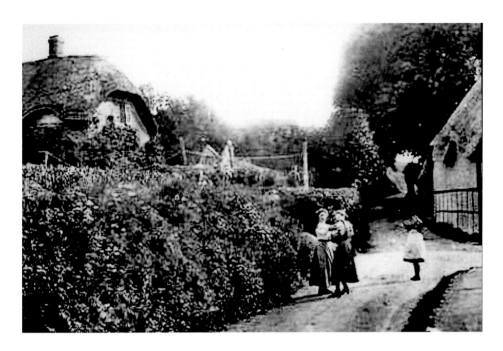

West Hendred: The Old Vicarage

Situated barely half a mile from East Hendred, West Hendred is a small and somewhat scattered village. The sepia view, dating from around 1912, shows cottages in Ginge Lane. The cottage on the extreme right, a seventeenth-century structure known as 'The Old Vicarage', is still extant, as shown in the lower picture. It is of box-frame construction with a thatched roof, the lower panels being filled with brickwork infill. The shed or outhouse at the south end of the building is clad in horizontal weatherboarding.

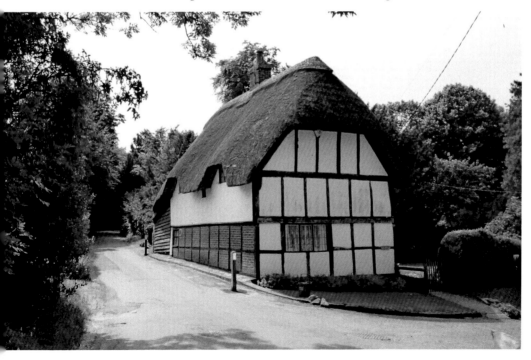

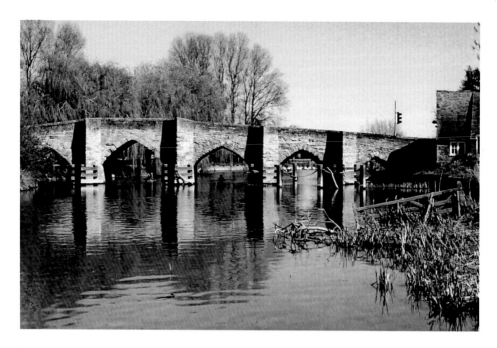

Envoi

Two final views of the Vale of the White Horse. The upper picture shows the historic bridge across the River Thames at Newbridge in May 2013, while the lower view shows the Vicarage at Ardington in the following July. This attractive building, which can also be seen on page 9, probably dates from the late seventeenth or early eighteenth century.

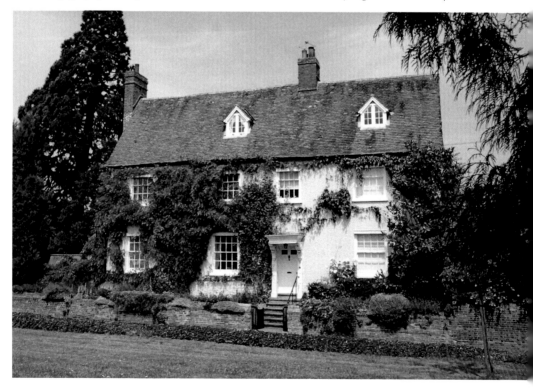